FRANK STEWART'S
WORLD OF
BRIDGE

To Roz and Paul,
a great team.

All the best to you!

Frank Stewart

FRANK STEWART'S
WORLD OF BRIDGE

FOREWORD BY JEFF RUBENS

SQUEEZE
BOOKS

ISBN: 1-58776-166-1
ISBN 13: 978-1-58776-166-9

Library of Congress Number: 2008931708

Bridge Book

Manufactured in the United States of America

VIVISPHERE
PUBLISHING
www.vivisphere.com

675 Dutchess Turnpike, Poughkeepsie, NY 12603
www.vivisphere.com (800) 724-1100

To my precious little Bessie and her Mama

Acknowledgments

Portions of this book are adapted from material that appeared in the ACBL's Bridge Bulletin and the OKbridge Spectator and are used with the kind permission of those publications. The material in "At My Club" is adapted from "Daily Bridge Club," my syndicated column, and appears with the kind permission of Tribune Media Services, Inc.

"Perfect Game," copyright 1998 by Bridge World Magazine Inc., appears with the kind permission of The Bridge World.

Contents

Foreword

Bridge offers spectacular variety and a remarkable mixture of technique and psychology. There is so much to see, so much to learn, and so much to ponder that a knowledgeable guide is indispensable. Indeed, it could be argued that the more such guides the merrier.

Frank Stewart is one of the valuable resources available to those who would increase their understanding and appreciation of the game. This collection of some of his best efforts offers both entertainment and advice, ways to improve both enjoyment and results. He displays his style and thus helps you to develop yours.

Do I agree with every idea expressed here? Of course not. It is a virtual impossibility that any two experienced analysts will hold the same views on each of a long list of bridge issues. However, as any knowledgeable player will confirm, one of the best ways to improve is to consider a variety of perspectives, evaluate them against personal experience, and draw conclusions. That in part explains the more-the-merrier bit mentioned earlier. When you formulate your list of expert observers, Frank Stewart should be on it.

Jeff Rubens

Publisher's Note

Mild-mannered Frank Stewart, a bridge columnist for Tribune Media Services, Inc., has some hard-edged observations to make, to wit:

"The standard of play has declined."

" ... explosion of professionalism in tournaments."

"... an influx of foreign experts who are dominating U.S. events."

In bidding, "System is supplanting judgment..."

Want to know what's behind each of these observations? Read on.

In addition, Stewart specializes in "over my shoulder" stories, where you get an insight into the way an expert views the bidding and play as they develop.

Provocative opinions, insightful observations, and entertaining stories. Boy, are you in the right place!

On demand...always in print..

Ron Garber
for SQueeZe Books

Introduction

"Yes, I live in my own little world. But it's okay; they know me here."
— a patient to his psychiatrist.

Come on into my world. I'm an extremely lucky man: I make my living writing about bridge, a game of great challenge and many rewards. Most of my journalist colleagues also teach, run a club, direct cruises or play professionally. I just write.

This book surveys some of my output. It includes "at my elbow" pieces in which you sit beside me during a deal and compare your decisions with mine. You won't agree with all my actions; it's a judgment game. My off-the-cuff analysis may not even be error-free; that's part of the game also. Still, I hope it will interest you to listen in on my thoughts

Since its inception, I have contributed to the Spectator, the on-line magazine that OKbridge, the excellent internet site, publishes for its members. In watching players from world-class to merely advanced cope with interesting and difficult deals on the net, I have found support for many of my opinions and have had to re-examine others. This book contains commentaries, mostly on modern bidding. You'll find that I am unimpressed with some of the recent "progress" in bidding theory. The qualities that once made reputations—soundness, discipline, good judgment and partnership trust—have been depreciated. I re-emphasize their role in winning bridge.

For 11 years I had the honor to collaborate with Alfred Sheinwold on his syndicated column. When Freddy died and I began to write the column alone, I knew it had to be entertaining as well as instructive. I envisioned something almost unprecedented: a bridge column with a running story line.

In 1982 I had published a short story about events at a club during the holidays. "Henrietta's Christmas" was the basis for my book "A Christmas Stocking" that introduced characters such as the myopic Minnie Bottoms, whose inability to tell kings from jacks drove her opponents crazy. In

"Daily Bridge Club," as my column is titled, the characters in my imaginary club live on, and others have joined them:

Unlucky Louie, who ascribes his disasters to bad luck despite all evidence to the contrary;

Cy the Cynic, the club philosopher, suspicious of everything and everybody;

Grapefruit, whose disposition is a cross between that of a traffic cop with heartburn and an untipped waiter. He makes his partners miserable;

Wendy, our feminist. Ask Wendy how many men it takes to wallpaper a room, and she'll say three if you slice them thinly.

The imagination of the incomparable Victor Mollo set a standard that won't be surpassed—who could outdo the Hideous Hog and the Rueful Rabbit?—but I do like my club, and this book is spiced with a few club episodes.

The book opens with an assessment of the state of our game. The world is changing rapidly, and a myriad of pastimes are available—many more than when bridge's popularity was at its height. To survive, bridge must compete. Many people have limited leisure time or lack the patience to learn games of complexity. Still, I continue to believe that there will always be bridge players.

Fayette AL
July 2008

PART the FIRST

The State of the Modern Game

Contract bridge, the culmination of a series of trick-taking card games that began with whist, was invented in 1925. Bridge is a game of endless variety: players with vast experience and world-class skills are always encountering something new. Its complex nature means that techniques, especially in bidding, continually evolve, and the socio-economic changes and technological advances of the past quarter-century have had their effects. Let me offer a half-dozen observations about the state of the modern game.

(1) The standard of play has declined.

"All players are poor players, including some good players."
— *Bob Hamman*

I often have lunch with my old music theory professor, a man of brilliance and erudition. A few years ago, prior to his retirement, I asked him whether students were coming to him as well prepared as those of my generation. He didn't reply; he just laughed.

Recently, I was on the phone with another bridge journalist who plays occasionally. He was telling me about his forays into club and sectional tournaments, and his comment was, "I can't believe how bad the level of play is."

The world is in an intellectual funk. I need not elaborate on the causes — they are evident — but the effects can be seen in most areas of human activity and have been adverse on demanding mental pastimes such as bridge. The bidding and play of the top echelon of experts may be steady, but the overall standard has fallen.

The American Contract Bridge League, which sponsors tournament competition in North America, has been unwittingly complicit. The ACBL is essentially a commercial venture that exists by giving its members what they want. When I began to play in tournaments in 1969, a weekend sectional had a Non-Masters Pairs on Friday evening, but the other events were open. Beginners were tried in the fire against experienced experts and had to improve or give up. Team events were Board-a-Match, at which new players struggled to break average. In time, the ACBL responded to that state of affairs with Swiss Teams, and later with an avalanche of Flighted, Stratified and Bracketed events. They made acquiring masterpoints easier – and reduced the incentive to get better.

Masterpoint inflation, incidentally, is rampant. The ACBL's system was never meant to accurately measure skill but seems to be out of control. In a Bracketed Knockout, for instance, the winners of the top bracket receive masterpoints based on the entire entry. The rich get ever richer.

Of all the players you know, half are below average. I wonder how today's "average" players would handle this dummy-play problem.

♠ A 9 8 2
♥ K 6 3
♦ 7 6
♣ K J 9 2

♠ Q J 10 6 4
♥ A 7 2
♦ K Q J
♣ 10 4

WEST	NORTH	EAST	SOUTH
	Pass	Pass	1♠
Pass	3♠	Pass	4♠
All Pass			

West leads the ♥J. Since the defenders threaten to set up a heart trick, declarer can't afford an early trump finesse. He should win the opening lead in dummy, saving the ♥ A as an entry, and lead a diamond. East wins the second diamond and returns a heart, and South wins and pitches dummy's last heart on the ♦J.

4

A trump finesse loses to East's king, a trump comes back, and South draws trumps and faces a club guess for the contract. But East, a passed hand, has shown the ♠K, ♥Q and ♦A, so West must have the ♣A.

Anyone can make this contract with a little concentration and care. How many would?

(2) The explosion of professionalism in tournaments is a symptom of a class system that is economically polarized.

Thirty-five years ago, when the Dallas Aces and C.C. Wei's Precision team were squaring off, the idea of a paid team was novel. But the U.S. is becoming a nation of haves and have nots: those who toil for minimum wage and no benefits and those who rake in big bucks. More people have more money than they know what to do with; more are able to hire a stable of bridge pros for fat retainers.

In major U.S. team events, almost all of the top 16 seeds now consist of a playing sponsor and a supporting cast of pros. The law of supply and demand operates: when the demand for pro services rises, fees will go up. The number of pros will increase.

This explains the influx of foreign experts who are dominating U.S. events. Of the 19 non-sponsor players in the semifinals of the 2007 Vanderbilt, 17 were of foreign extraction. One semifinalist team had two members of the reigning world champions from Italy; their opponents fielded the other four! Only the luck of the draw spared the ACBL from seeing the final of its "national" championship contested among six Italians and other foreigners.

(In the 2007 Vanderbilt final, both teams had woman captains; a winning Vanderbilt team had a woman member for the first time since 1963. Only two women had ever played on a U.S. Bermuda Bowl Team, and none since 1965, but in 2001 Rose Meltzer and her five pros *won* the Bowl. Few would deny that the quality of play among women has improved, but these results surely reflect the impact of professionalism. As an aside: my impression, though I have no statistics to support it, is that women's events are losing some of their popularity.)

With the foreign experts have come unfamiliar systems and problems with communication and inadequate disclosure. But that's another story.

(3) System is supplanting judgment as the dominant factor in bidding.

Modern theorists have come up with bidding methods of frightening efficiency. Notable are "relay" systems in which bids are artificial and the auction amounts to a question-and-answer session. One player makes a series of minimum bids; his partner describes his hand in response to the "relays," after which the relayer places the contract. Relayer's hand may be unknown, and if he is declarer, the defenders' task can be baffling.

The striking feature of other systems is their complexity. They may brandish opening bids with multiple meanings or opening passes that show strength. Whether these systems are superior in theory is questionable, but they gain in practice by sowing confusion and placing opponents in unfamiliar situations.

Bizarre systems and conventions are regulated in U.S. tournaments, but the emphasis on system has still increased due to the rise of the "two-over-one-game-force" style in which an auction such as 1♠-2♦ is forcing to game. This allows for leisurely investigation of game and slam.

♠ A 9 7 6 3	♠ K
♥ K 9 5 3	♥ Q 6 4 2
♦ K	♦ A Q J 10 9 8
♣ K 10 3	♣ Q 6

WEST	EAST
1♠	2♦ (1)
2♥	3♥
3NT	

(1) forcing to game

Two-over-one advocates can point to this result. East's 3♥ was forcing, and West suggested 3NT even though he risked finding a dummy with a low singleton spade. East, with club help, weakish hearts and a source of tricks in diamonds, was happy to pass. A 4♥ contract might have failed, but West made two overtricks at 3NT after a club lead.

I believe that two-over-one is overrated, but I'm not blind to its gains. "Standard" bidders would have trouble reaching 3NT. East would usually

6

jump to 4♥ over 2♥ . Only a cautious East might allow for the possibility of 3NT and try a "fourth-suit" bid of 3♣ over 2♥. Then if West bid 3NT, East might pass.

Cy the Cynic says that everyone makes bad bids, but having a system allows us to make them on purpose. A weakness of two-over-one—by no means its only one—is seen here:

♠ K 9 5 4 3	♠ Q 10
♥ A Q J 2	♥ K
♦ A K	♦ Q 10 8 6 4 3
♣ 8 6	♣ A K 5 2

WEST	EAST
1♠	2♦
2♥	2NT
3♦	3♠
3NT	Pass

Too much "leisurely investigation" came to grief. East-West missed a good slam because neither player made a descriptive, value bid. I often see such auctions when even experienced players use two-over-one.

A strength of two-over-one is its attempt to narrowly define as many sequences as possible, but it's risky to play any elaborate system that you and your partner haven't thoroughly discussed. Your system may be superior in theory, but in practice you'll lose on misunderstandings.

The emphasis on system disturbs me most because I fear players think learning a system will guarantee good results. (Today, if you hire a pro partner, his first move may be to teach you his system with all the trimmings.) Players neglect to develop skills such as hand evaluation in the bidding and counting and drawing inferences in the play.

Another indication of the decline of judgment is the influence of the Law of Total Tricks. Few readers will need to be told about this concept, which was enunciated by Jean-René Vernes in a 1969 article. After Larry Cohen's best-selling book in 1992, players began to rely on the Law in making competitive decisions.

The LOTT is most accurate at low levels—at higher levels, it is at the mercy of freak distributions—but at any level, judgment must accompany its use. Players must consider the presence of double fits and the location of minor honors. Many players forget that the "Law" is not a law, only a statistical observation. It should be a guideline and no more.

Theorists have continued to scrutinize the LOTT. Some have questioned its utility. Recent books have suggested alternative methods of assessing trick-taking potential.

(4) It's a bidder's game.

Nowadays, players are less terrified of telephone-number penalties. They open light, respond on a whim and compete actively. (In this book, I note that light opening bids in conjunction with the two-over-one style can impede constructive bidding.)

Players have always known the value of preemption, but the philosophy of modern bidding stresses it. Given a free run, capable pairs will often reach accurate contracts. So many players employ a hyperactive preemptive style. They enter the auction freely, wielding an array of obstructive—really, destructive—gadgets.

For a perspective of modern bridge, look at this deal from the 2006 World Open Teams final.

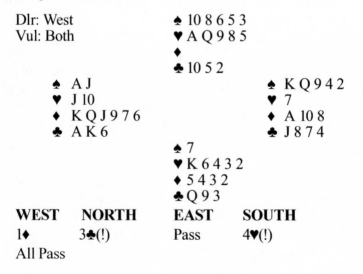

Dlr: West
Vul: Both

North: ♠ 10 8 6 5 3 ♥ A Q 9 8 5 ♦ ♣ 10 5 2

West: ♠ A J ♥ J 10 ♦ K Q J 9 7 6 ♣ A K 6

East: ♠ K Q 9 4 2 ♥ 7 ♦ A 10 8 ♣ J 8 7 4

South: ♠ 7 ♥ K 6 4 3 2 ♦ 5 4 3 2 ♣ Q 9 3

WEST	NORTH	EAST	SOUTH
1♦	3♣(!)	Pass	4♥(!)
All Pass			

North's 3♣ conventionally showed length in both major suits. East had no obvious call, and South preempted with 4♥. West might have doubled, but no action was safe: East might have held nothing. So West passed, and though East may have suspected his opponents were stealing, he passed also. The result was down one after West led the ♣K—South had only three losers but only nine winners—and East-West got 100 points in exchange for their slam.

In the replay, West opened 1♣, merely showing a strong hand. North-South did bid hearts, but West had a chance to show his diamonds, and East-West reached 6♦ and made it for a 15-IMP gain.

Sensible preemption will gain, but some players are apt to carry the destructive approach to an extreme. I fear this is an outgrowth of society's yen for instant gratification. Bridge is still a partnership game, and preempts should be reasonably descriptive; but the trend toward unilateral and undisciplined actions has even intruded into the area of weak two-bids. A columnist in the ACBL's magazine wrote that almost all experts would open 2♠ as dealer on

♠ Q J 10 8 6 4   ♥ J 8 6 4   ♦   ♣ K 8 3.

If that assertion is true—and the magazine published it as if it were fact, not opinion—I am reminded of a bumper sticker I saw: "Where are we going, and why am I in this handbasket?"

(5) The double has acquired new meanings.

How do I double thee? Let me count the ways: negative, responsive, maximal, cooperative, support, and more. Experts are increasingly treating a double as a conventional tool or as a flexible call to say, "I want to act but have no clear action; partner, do something intelligent." I'm tempted to predict that by 2020, penalty doubles will be extinct.

IMPs, N-S vulnerable

WEST	NORTH	EAST	SOUTH
			Pass
Pass	1♦	1♥	Dbl
2♥	Dbl	Pass	?

♠ A 8 6 3
♥ K 8 3
♦ Q J 4 2
♣ 10 4

When an expert panel considered this problem, nobody was sure what North's double showed. (What should South bid? I thought 4♦ was best; most panelists preferred 2NT.)

Matchpoints, neither side vulnerable

WEST	NORTH	EAST	SOUTH
	1♣	Pass	1♥
1♠	2♣	2♠	?

♠ A 7 6
♥ Q J 10 9 4
♦ K 8 7 2
♣ 5

A panel's plurality choice was a double: "for penalty but cooperative." If that sounds contradictory to you, I sympathize.

Many experts recommend competitive doubles that strike me as esoteric.

WEST	NORTH	EAST	SOUTH
	1♠	2♦	Dbl (1)
Pass	2♠	3♦	Dbl (2)

(1) negative
(2) ?

When this auction arose in an internet game with commentary, the commentator said that South's second double was "card-showing." Would you wonder, as I did, what South was supposed to do if he held

♠ 7　♥ K 10 7 4　♦ K 9 7 2　♣ A J 8 3?

(6) The internet has had a major positive effect on bridge.

Has it ever! The game now conjoins the world like never before. Sites such as OK bridge and Bridge Base Online let you compete against players all over. (On-line play has many advantages: for example, insufficient bids and opening leads out of turn are eliminated.) If you live in New York, you can fashion a partnership with a Californian. Major tournaments are broadcast with expert commentary, and archives are available. Eventually, world championships will be conducted via the net.

Do you think playing bridge at a computer renders the art of "table presence" obsolete? I recall a deal from before internet bridge became a business.

```
Dlr: South        ♠ Q 9 7
Vul: N-S          ♥ 9 7 5 3 2
                  ♦ A J 7
                  ♣ 10 4
   ♠ K J 10 4                      ♠ 8 6 5 3 2
   ♥ 8                             ♥ K 10
   ♦ Q 9 2                         ♦ 8 3
   ♣ K Q J 8 3                     ♣ 9 7 6 2
                  ♠ A
                  ♥ A Q J 6 4
                  ♦ K 10 6 5 4
                  ♣ A 5
```

SOUTH	WEST	NORTH	EAST
1♥	Dbl	2♥	Pass
3♦	Pass	4♥	Pass
4♠	Pass	5♦	Pass
6♥	All Pass		

I was North, and South and I stretched to 6♥. It would have been a better slam on any lead other than the actual one: the ♣ K. My partner took his ace and led a diamond to dummy's jack. This play produced the three from East, a warm glow in my heart and a simple and rueful comment on the screen from West:

:(

South wasn't home yet. He led a trump from dummy and was obliged to take a view when East played the ten. If East had the king left, a finesse would land the slam. If West had the king, South needed to play the ace. Even if the king didn't fall, South would be safe if West had a hand such as KJ104,K8,Q92,KQ83: South could shift back to diamonds and get rid of a club from dummy before West ruffed in.

11

South judged to put up the ♥A. West followed low, and East ruffed the third diamond and returned a club. Down one.

South may have thought his play was best, but his table presence—or computer presence—was lacking. West's indiscreet :(was a giveaway. When East couldn't beat the ♦J, West obviously thought South was about to wrap up the slam—hence West couldn't have the ♥ K.

The computer revolution has had other benefits. Programs allow players to generate a set of deals with any parameters, letting them practice their bidding after, say, a 1NT opening. "Simulations" let analysts reach definitive answers to bidding problems.

Programs such as William Bailey's "Deep Finesse" have rendered the double-dummy problem obsolete. I was asked for the solution to this taxing problem.

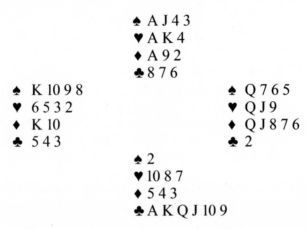

```
              ♠ A J 4 3
              ♥ A K 4
              ♦ A 9 2
              ♣ 8 7 6
♠ K 10 9 8                    ♠ Q 7 6 5
♥ 6 5 3 2                     ♥ Q J 9
♦ K 10                        ♦ Q J 8 7 6
♣ 5 4 3                       ♣ 2
              ♠ 2
              ♥ 10 8 7
              ♦ 5 4 3
              ♣ A K Q J 10 9
```

Can South make 5♣ on the lead of the ♠10?

I sensed the need to play the ♠J, rectifying the count for the end game and preventing West from shifting to a heart and ruining South's possible tenace. But then lines of play diverged.

I gave up early, but "Deep Finesse" solved the problem in two seconds. Suppose East takes the ♠Q and shifts to a trump. South cashes five trumps, pitching a heart and a spade from dummy. He leads to the ♥K, discards a diamond on the ♠A and leads a spade. East is down to ♥QJ and ♦QJ8. If he pitches a diamond, South ruffs, ducks a diamond and scores two diamond tricks; if East pitches a heart honor, South throws a diamond. West wins and leads a diamond, but South takes the ace, cashes the ♥A and still has a trump entry to his hand for the high ♥10.

Say East shifts to a diamond at the second trick. If West plays the ten, South can effectively win or duck. Suppose he wins. He continues with the ♠A and a spade ruff and cashes four trumps, discarding a heart from dummy. He goes to the ♥K and leads the last spade. East must discard from ♥QJ ♦QJ. If he discards a heart, South discards a diamond and scores his ♥10 at the end; if East discards a diamond, South ruffs and leads a diamond, making dummy high.

If instead South ducks the first diamond and West shifts to a heart, South wins, discards a diamond on the ♠A, ruffs a spade, and cashes four trumps, discarding a heart from dummy. He goes to the ♥K and leads the last spade, and East is stuck.

If West plays the king on the trick-two diamond shift, South must take the ace and run all his trumps but one. West must save three spades, else South can set up a spade trick in dummy, and hence must pitch two hearts. East then gets squeezed in the red suits.

Finally, let East shift to the ♥Q at trick two. South takes the ace, discards a diamond on the ♠A, ruffs a spade and leads a diamond: ten, ace. South ruffs a spade and cashes his last trump, throwing a heart from dummy.

East has room for three cards. If he holds ♥J, ♦QJ, South takes the ♥A and leads a diamond, and West must win and concede the 13th trick to the ♥10; if instead East comes down to one diamond, South leads a diamond, and dummy is high. In this variation, West can't gain by putting up the ♦K on the first diamond. At the end, East must allow West to be endplayed in hearts or must give dummy a trick with the ♦9.

Can programs that find single-dummy solutions to a problem be far behind?

Over the past 30 years, our game has seen changes and endured upheavals: an aging bridge population (the median age of ACBL members has risen); a widening gulf between the weekly social-outlet games at Aunt Tillie's and the tournament world; difficulties marketing the game due to the lack of big-money events and television exposure (poker is easily televised, bridge is not); a few well publicized cheating scandals.

Yet, I don't doubt that the greatest of all card games will go on. The positive effects of card-playing on mental acuity are hard to ignore when a recent study showed that a significant part of the population will eventually be at risk from Alzheimer's disease. Another study showed that playing bridge improves the immune system!

Part of bridge's salvation may lie with the internet; I see young players there. But the game also has powerful advocates. In November 2005, the New York Times ran a remarkable Op-Ed piece by Sharon Osberg, a world champion and mentor to Bill Gates and Warren Buffett. Osberg noted that though poker is popular, bridge has more to offer. She announced an initiative backed by Gates and Buffett for bridge education in schools.

I believe bridge is headed for a renaissance. People will want games that offer more challenge as well as sociability. But we shall see.

Sit Beside Me

In a local Knockout Teams, both sides are vulnerable, and I'm in third position with

♠ Q 5 4 3
♥ A Q 10 6 4 2
♦ 7
♣ A Q

After two passes, I open 1♥, and my partner raises to 2♥. After a pass at my right, I must decide how high to go.

There are two approaches: one is to count my points, but it's hard to say how many points my hand is worth. I have 14 high-card points, and the fifth and sixth heart are worth perhaps a point and a half each after partner has raised. I can probably ruff my fourth spade in dummy if I need to, but then the ♠Q may be of little value; and the ♣Q may or may not win a trick. I'd say the hand is worth 17 points; other players would value it differently.

An easier method is to visualize typical minimum hands for partner and commit to game if I can construct one that will make game a good shot. If he has 64,K953,86542,76 (a subminimum), I'll have about a 50% chance; and 86,K95,86542,K93 will give me a good chance.

Since partner's spade holding may be the key, I could test the water with 2♠. That bid would ask him to go to game with any sound raise or with a fair raise that contained values in spades. I'd avoid game opposite an ill-fitting hand such as 642,J93,KJ86,K86, but might reach game opposite a suitable minimum such as K2,K953,6542,864.

If the game were matchpoints or if this were a short match, I might try 2♠. But this is a 36-board match, and the odds favor bidding close vulnerable games: I have more IMPs to gain if I make than to lose if I go down. If I bid 2♠, I'd give the opponents information about my hand. I might stretch to try for game with 2♠ on a less-promising hand. Since I have a sound invitation, I just blast into 4♥ and hope for the best.

West leads the ♠A, and dummy is not encouraging.

```
            ♠ 10 9 2
            ♥ J 9 3
            ♦ A Q 10 4 3
            ♣ 7 5


            ♠ Q 5 4 3
            ♥ A Q 10 6 4 2
            ♦ 7
            ♣ A Q
```

WEST	NORTH	EAST	SOUTH
	Pass	Pass	1♥
Pass	2♥	Pass	4♥
All Pass			

East signals with the ♠8, and West leads another spade to the king. Back comes the ♠J, and West ruffs my queen and shifts to the ♦9, forcing me to take an early view.

I wonder if I can place the cards. I must assume East has the ♥K so I can pick up the trumps; to play West for the bare king now would be a deep position.

What about the major-suit kings? If West has the ♦K and East has the ♣K, I can't go wrong; if the position of those two kings is reversed, I'm always down. If East has both kings, I must put up the ♦A, pick up the trumps with a finesse, ruff my last spade and finesse in clubs. But wait: East, a passed hand, has shown the ♠KJ, and I'm assuming he has the ♥K, so I can't play him for both minor-suit kings. That would mean he passed with 13 points.

What about both kings with West? Then I have to finesse with the ♦Q now. That must be right. If the diamond finesse loses, the club finesse would have lost also (assuming the ♥K is onside).

Dummy's ♦Q wins, and I discard the ♣Q on the ♦A and let the ♥9 ride. When both defenders follow low, I can lead another trump and claim. The full deal:

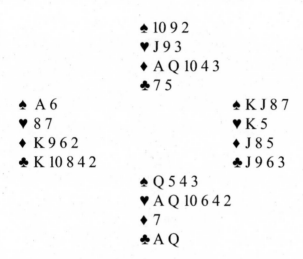

♠ 10 9 2
♥ J 9 3
♦ A Q 10 4 3
♣ 7 5

♠ A 6
♥ 8 7
♦ K 9 6 2
♣ K 10 8 4 2

♠ K J 8 7
♥ K 5
♦ J 8 5
♣ J 9 6 3

♠ Q 5 4 3
♥ A Q 10 6 4 2
♦ 7
♣ A Q

At the other table, South settled for 2♠ over North's 2♥, and North tried 3♦ next. Since this was not the bid South wanted to hear, he signed off at 3♥. The opening lead was a club, and South took ten tricks without breathing hard. It was a lucky gain for us.

As I See It

Opening Ingredients

Forty-five years ago, experts such as Alvin Roth and Ira Rubin were advocating super-sound openings. Some of their first-seat passes were startling: a hand such as Ax,xxx,Ax,KJxxxx wasn't good enough to open. This style had successes but also spectacular and well publicized disasters, and the backlash began. Nowadays, more players seem to think the ingredients for an opening bid are eye of newt, toe of frog and 11 random high-card points.

Every player has his own idea of what constitutes an opening bid, but the key factors should be winners and Quick Tricks. To initiate an auction when your prospects on defense are uncertain makes little sense; to undertake to fulfill a contract when you lack playing tricks makes none.

I was watching a strong IMP game on OKbridge, and within 20 minutes I saw three deals that hinged on the opening bid. First:

```
Dlr: North        ♠ 7 5
Vul: None         ♥ Q 10 4 3
                  ♦ A Q 10 9 5
                  ♣ K 4
    ♠ A J 10 9               ♠ K 8 4 3
    ♥ J 9 5 2               ♥ 8 7 6
    ♦ J 6                   ♦ K 8 3 2
    ♣ A 8 2                 ♣ 10 6
                  ♠ Q 6 2
                  ♥ A K
                  ♦ 7 4
                  ♣ Q J 9 7 5 3
```

North thought his plus features (good five-card suit, two tens) outweighed his minuses (skimpy high-card values, possible rebid problems); he opened 1♦. Alas, he caught South with a decent 12-count, and since South's 2♣ response was forcing to game, the auction was:

WEST	NORTH	EAST	SOUTH
	1♦	Pass	2♣
Pass	2♦	Pass	2NT
Pass	3♥	Pass	3NT
All Pass			

After North's 3♥ warned against notrump, South's 3NT was foolhardy. If South had weaseled with 4♣, North might have passed ("game-forcing" auctions shouldn't force to an 11-trick contract), but even 4♣ would have been shaky.

This illustrates a problem with wide-ranging opening bids. Poor games result because responder can't know what he needs for game. If North passed, I'd expect South to open 1♣, and North to respond in a red suit and raise South's 2♣ rebid to 3♣—and there they'd rest for a prosaic plus.

Dlr: North	♠ J 5 3	
Vul: None	♥ Q 7 5 3	
	♦ K Q 5	
	♣ A J 7	

♠ A 7		♠ Q 10 8 6
♥ A 10 8 6		♥ J 9 4 2
♦ A 9 8 7 2		♦ 10 4
♣ Q 3		♣ K 10 5

	♠ K 9 4 2	
	♥ K	
	♦ J 6 3	
	♣ 9 8 6 4 2	

WEST	NORTH	EAST	SOUTH
	1♣	Pass	1♠
Dbl	Pass	2♥	3♣
Pass	3♠	Pass	4♣
All Pass			

I suspect you and I would also have opened North's barren 13-point hand despite the notable lack of winners. When South competed, perhaps questionably, with 3♣, and North huddled, my mind telegraphed an urgent

20

message: "Pass. Trust your partner." Alas, the message didn't arrive. North unwisely tried 3♠, and North-South landed at 4♣—and were lucky not to be socked for -500. With about as many losers as winners, North went three down.

Finally, I saw a successful opening bid:

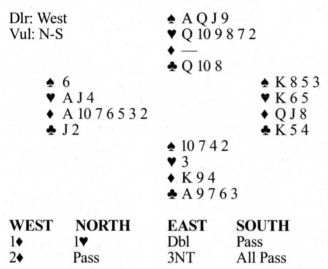

Dlr: West
Vul: N-S

♠ A Q J 9
♥ Q 10 9 8 7 2
♦ —
♣ Q 10 8

♠ 6
♥ A J 4
♦ A 10 7 6 5 3 2
♣ J 2

♠ K 8 5 3
♥ K 6 5
♦ Q J 8
♣ K 5 4

♠ 10 7 4 2
♥ 3
♦ K 9 4
♣ A 9 7 6 3

WEST	NORTH	EAST	SOUTH
1♦	1♥	Dbl	Pass
2♦	Pass	3NT	All Pass

West would have preferred his long suit were a major, but he did have winners, two aces and an easy rebid. East, no doubt, would have liked an ace to leap to 3NT, but he couldn't stay out of game with a good diamond fit. South led a club, and East wrapped up +430 when the diamond finesse won.

If West passed as dealer, I'd expect North to open 1♥ and South to respond 1♠. West would overcall 2♦, but East-West wouldn't reach game and might sell out to a North-South spade partial.

Which of the opening bids do you like best?

At My Club

Dlr: East
Vul: N-S

```
              ♠ K Q 9
              ♥ 6 3
              ♦ K Q J 7 3
              ♣ 7 4 2
  ♠ 10 3 2                    ♠ A J 7 6
  ♥ 7 4                       ♥ 9 8 2
  ♦ 9 5 2                     ♦ A 10 6
  ♣ J 10 9 6 3                ♣ A 8 5
              ♠ 8 5 4
              ♥ A K Q J 10 5
              ♦ 8 4
              ♣ K Q
```

WEST	NORTH	EAST	SOUTH
		1♣	1♥
Pass	2♦	Pass	4♥
All Pass			

Unlucky Louie, one of the regulars at my club, attributes all his bad results to bad luck despite overwhelming evidence to the contrary. When I found Louie in the club lounge, he and his checkbook were having a tag-team match against a pile of unpaid bills.

"Look at this," Louie said glumly. "The Water Board wants their money—they say they've carried me longer than my mother did. And here's a letter from the power company saying they'd be delighted if I paid up—but I will be if I don't."

That afternoon, Louie tried to prop up his bank balance in the penny Chicago game, but he wasn't delighted after this deal. As South, he leaped to 4♥ when North offered encouragement with a diamond bid. West led the ♣J.

East took the ace, dropping Louie's queen, and did well to shift to a low spade. West's ten forced out the queen, killing dummy's late entry to the diamonds. Louie drew trumps and led a diamond, but West signaled with the deuce. East therefore let dummy's king win, but when Louie came back to his ♣ K and led another diamond to the queen, East won and led a club. Louie ruffed but lost two spades for down one, slipping deeper into the hole.

"Nice defense," Louie said grudgingly.

How would you play 4♥?

Louie's contract was unbeatable. After Louie draws trumps, he takes the ♣K before leading a diamond to the king. He then ruffs dummy's last club and leads another diamond to the queen. When East takes the ace, he has no more clubs. All East can do is to cash the ♠A, holding Louie to 10 tricks.

PART the SECOND

Sit Beside Me

In the 5th Century B.C. the Greek philosopher Zeno of Elea contrived paradoxes that perplexed thinkers for an era. (One was "The Arrow," proposing that motion is impossible since even an arrow in flight must be located somewhere — and therefore must be at rest — at any given instant.) Bridge has its own paradoxes. Can 11 winners and three losers occupy the same 13 tricks?

In a Sectional Swiss Teams, neither side is vulnerable, and I'm South, the dealer, with:

♠ A 7
♥ 8 6 3
♦ J 9 8 7 5 3 2
♣ 6

I expect my counterpart may open with a lusty 3♦, but my temperament won't let me preempt with a suit that may contain only three winners, and I do have a couple of possible defensive tricks against a major-suit contract. I pass and, as it happens, East-West stay out. My partner opens 1♣, I respond 1♦ and he jumps to 2NT.

I'm not sure what we can make, if anything, but I can't pass. If I were using a method such as the Wolff signoff, I could handle this hand. I'd bid 3♣, conventionally forcing 3♦ from North, and then I'd pass or raise to 4♦ to invite game. But since he and I haven't discuss this sequence, all I can do is try 3♦, natural and forcing.

North persists with 3NT. I suppose we might make it—he might hold K96,AK4,A104,KQ105—but to pass looks against the odds. If 3NT fails, it may be by a lot, and at IMPs, I can afford to play game at a minor suit. Right or wrong, I pull to 4♦. In theory, we're in a game-forcing auction, but if North doesn't like his hand for diamonds, I don't expect him to lift to an 11-trick contract.

He thinks it over and bids 5♦. Everyone passes, West leads the ♠Q and I wait to see whether I've made a good decision.

```
        ♠ 9 6 5 2
        ♥ A K 4
        ♦ A K
        ♣ A J 5 4


        ♠ A 7
        ♥ 8 6 3
        ♦ J 9 8 7 5 3 2
        ♣ 6
```

WEST	NORTH	EAST	SOUTH
			Pass
Pass	1♣	Pass	1♦
Pass	2NT	Pass	3♦
Pass	3NT	Pass	4♦
Pass	5♦	All Pass	

I don't mind North's descriptive 2NT rebid, suppressing his spades, but it seems he could have bid 3♥ over 3♦, showing concentrated strength. His 3NT risked playing there opposite a singleton spade.

A spade opening lead would have beaten 3NT, and any lead might have beaten it, but I shouldn't worry about a contract I don't have to play. At 5♦ I see three losers: a spade, a heart and a trump. I need something good to happen. The ♦Q may fall, or a defender may have ♣ KQx so I can set up dummy's jack with two ruffs.

Since I foresee one other chance, I lead to the ♣ A at the second trick, ruff a club and concede a spade. East wins and returns a trump to dummy's ace.

I ruff another club and lead another trump, on which West shows out. That's good news and bad news: the defense has a trump trick, but for

East to hold it is to my advantage. I ruff a spade, lead to the ♥A and ruff dummy's last club as both defenders follow.

I think I'm home now. I go back to the ♥K and lead the last spade at the 12th trick. East has no more spades, but whether he ruffs in with his ♦Q or discards, I'm bound to score my ♦J to fulfill the contract. He discards, I ruff and the defenders' heart and trump winners clash at trick 13. A red-suit opening lead would have beaten me. The full deal:

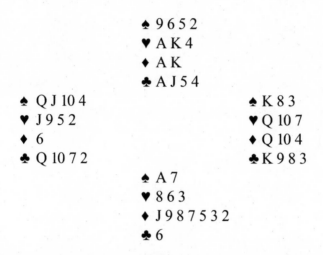

```
              ♠ 9 6 5 2
              ♥ A K 4
              ♦ A K
              ♣ A J 5 4
  ♠ Q J 10 4               ♠ K 8 3
  ♥ J 9 5 2                ♥ Q 10 7
  ♦ 6                      ♦ Q 10 4
  ♣ Q 10 7 2               ♣ K 9 8 3
              ♠ A 7
              ♥ 8 6 3
              ♦ J 9 8 7 5 3 2
              ♣ 6
```

Mathematicians disposed of some of Zeno's paradoxes by defining the "sum of an infinite series." I disposed of 5♦ with a "coup en passant" – provided I began to take ruffs in my hand immediately.

You wouldn't guess the contract at the other table. The bidding started 1♣ -1♦ again, but North didn't want to suppress his spade suit (such as it was) and was afraid to jump. He rebid 1♠. Some partnerships play this sequence as forcing, but South saw the storm clouds of a misfit and passed, playing for a plus score. He got one: although East found a trump lead, North assembled seven tricks for +80.

In a Sectional Swiss Teams, neither side is vulnerable, and I'm West, the dealer, with

♠ Q J 3
♥ A 8 3
♦ 9 3 2
♣ A 10 7 3

After I and North pass, my partner tables a red "Stop" card and then a 2♠ card. That's a weak two-bid. South duly studies his hand for several seconds, then produces a 4♥ card. That's a strong bid; a preempt over a preempt doesn't exist. South expects to make 4♥ if North has a useful card or two.

I'm tempted to sacrifice at 4♠. I estimate East can take eight tricks, and -300 will show a profit if 4♥ makes for +420. The Law of Total Tricks inevitably flits across my mind. If East has a singleton heart, which seems likely, each side has nine trumps, and 18 total tricks are available. If 4♥ makes, we're down two at 4♠ – or so says the "Law."

At matchpoints I might back my judgment and save, but at IMPs the odds aren't good. I might lose 8 IMPs if I'm wrong, and I'd gain only 4 IMPs if I were right. I'm nowhere near sure South can make 4♥: I have a good defensive hand — even the ♣ 10 may be a factor — and a good opening lead. Moreover, I suspect dummy will be a wasteland, and South may have problems getting there to lead toward his high cards. I pass and lead the ♠Q.

```
                    ♠ K 6 4
                    ♥ 6 5
                    ♦ J 10 6 4
                    ♣ Q J 4 2
    ♠ Q J 3
    ♥ A 8 3              N
    ♦ 9 3 2         W  ─┼─  E
    ♣ A 10 7 3          S
```

WEST	NORTH	EAST	SOUTH
Pass	Pass	2♠	4♥
All Pass			

Dummy has about what I expected. That ♠K is nice to see. It's worthless to declarer, and since East doesn't have it, he'll have an honor somewhere else.

My ♠Q wins, and I continue with the ♠J. South ruffs and leads the ♥K. I take the ace, and East plays the jack. Now all I must do is exit safely and let South play from his hand. I have my fingers on another spade—but then it occurs to me that I'm spending an exit card I may need later. Instead I get out with my ♥8, making sure South must win in his hand.

South draws my last trump and leads the ♣ K. I duck, and East plays the six. When declarer leads the ♣ 5 next, I can play East for three clubs and take the ace. Now I lead my last spade. The full deal:

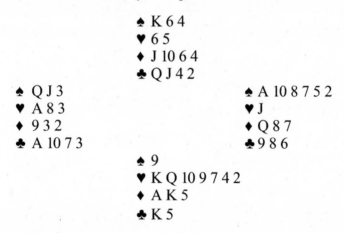

```
                        ♠ K 6 4
                        ♥ 6 5
                        ♦ J 10 6 4
                        ♣ Q J 4 2
        ♠ Q J 3                         ♠ A 10 8 7 5 2
        ♥ A 8 3                         ♥ J
        ♦ 9 3 2                         ♦ Q 8 7
        ♣ A 10 7 3                      ♣ 9 8 6
                        ♠ 9
                        ♥ K Q 10 9 7 4 2
                        ♦ A K 5
                        ♣ K 5
```

South ruffs but must lead diamonds from his hand and lose the setting trick to East's queen.

If I carelessly lead a spade at the fourth trick, South ruffs, draw trumps and leads the ♣ K and another club. I win but must give dummy a club trick or declarer a free finesse in diamonds.

The "Law" was on target here, but only in theory. We'd be down two at 4♠, and South had ten tricks at 4♥ with the winning diamond finesse. Alas, he couldn't reach dummy to take it. Deals are played at the table, not in theory.

In a Life Master Pairs final, both sides are vulnerable, and I'm West with:

♠ A 10 8 6 3
♥ J 5
♦ Q 9 5
♣ A 10 6

North deals and opens 1♥, and South responds 2♦. They aren't using a game-forcing 2/1 style; nevertheless, to overcall 2♠ is way too rich for me. I pass, North rebids 2♥, South tries 2NT and North lifts to 3NT.

I make the textbook lead of the ♠6 and see

```
              ♠ 9 5
              ♥ A Q 10 9 6 4
              ♦ A 8
              ♣ K J 3
 ♠ A 10 8 6 3
 ♥ J 5              N
 ♦ Q 9 5       W  +  E
 ♣ A 10 6          S
```

WEST	NORTH	EAST	SOUTH
	1♥	Pass	2♦
Pass	2♥	Pass	2NT
Pass	3NT	All Pass	

East plays the ♠J, and South wins with the king. Either he or East could hold the queen. South then leads a heart to the queen. I wait hopefully for East to produce the king and fire back a spade, but he follows with the eight. Dummy next leads the ♣ 3: eight, queen ... and I take the ace. What now?

South should have about 11 points. I know eight of them: the ♠K, ♥K and ♣ Q. (East won't have ducked the ♥K; he'd be eager to win a trick and return a spade.) So South has one more good card. I can see two possible hands for him. One is:

♠ K x x   ♥ K x x   ♦ K x x x   ♣ Q x x;

the other is:

32

♠ K Q x ♥ K x x ♦ J 10 x x ♣ Q x x.

Which hand should I play South for?

I must think carefully because many matchpoints may be at stake. If South has the second hand, all I can do is exit with a diamond or a club and watch declarer take six hearts, two clubs, a diamond and a spade. We'll be -630, and our matchpoint score won't be good. Many North-Souths will play at 4♥ when South shows his support or North jumps to 4♥ over 2NT. North will lose a diamond, a club and a spade for +620.

I may as well play South for the first hand since we'll have a chance to score well. Anyhow, maybe he has the king of the suit he bid. I lay down the ♠A. East comes through by unblocking his queen — a lovely sight to see — and I take the ♠10 and two more spades for down one. The full deal:

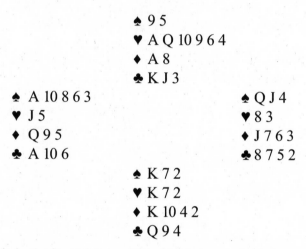

```
              ♠ 9 5
              ♥ A Q 10 9 6 4
              ♦ A 8
              ♣ K J 3
♠ A 10 8 6 3                    ♠ Q J 4
♥ J 5                           ♥ 8 3
♦ Q 9 5                         ♦ J 7 6 3
♣ A 10 6                        ♣ 8 7 5 2
              ♠ K 7 2
              ♥ K 7 2
              ♦ K 10 4 2
              ♣ Q 9 4
```

South had nine tricks and would have cashed them at IMPs. In a strong matchpoint event, he judged that +600 would be a poor result since many North-South pairs would be +620. So South risked his contract to steal a club trick, trying for +630.

If I'd cashed the ♠A and found declarer with K-Q-x, he'd have made two overtricks, but my defense had more matchpoints to gain than to lose.

In a local Knockout event, my team has managed to reach the final. At the half we're trailing by 20 IMPs, our opponents having given away nothing at either table. Early in the second half, I'm South, the dealer, with:

♠ K Q 10 8 4
♥ A K J 10 4
♦ —
♣ 8 7 2

Both sides are vulnerable. I open 1♠, North responds 2♦, I rebid 2♥ and he jumps to 3♠. After his response at the two level, his jump preference is forcing, and I can't bid less than 4♠. The question is whether I should cue-bid 4♥ on the way: in our "Standard" methods, North's 3♠ neither showed nor denied slam aspirations.

When slam is in the picture, many experts use "obligatory" cue-bids under game. (See also pages 133, 221 and 228) Personally, I wouldn't consider showing my ♥A if I'd opened with:

♠ K J 10 8 4 ♥ A Q J 10 4 ♦ — ♣ J 7 2.

With my actual hand? I don't like my diamond void, but I do have good trumps and a source of tricks in hearts. So I shrug mentally and try 4♥, and partner replies with a 5♣ cue-bid. He's gone past 4♠, so his interest must be serious. Surely I'll have a play for slam.

When I bid 6♠, my partner huddles for three minutes. East-West are fidgety by the time he finally bids 7♠. I hope he knows what he's doing. Everyone passes, and West leads the ♣ K.

♠ A 7 2
♥ 5 2
♦ A K J 5 4 3
♣ A 3

♠ K Q 10 8 4
♥ A K J 10 4
♦ —
♣ 8 7 2

34

WEST	NORTH	EAST	SOUTH
			1♠
Pass	2♦	Pass	2♥
Pass	3♠	Pass	4♥
Pass	5♣	Pass	6♠
Pass	7♠	All Pass	

I have a play for it, but I'd just as soon be at 6♠. When North bid 7♠, I expect he was thinking mostly about our 20-IMP deficit.

I start faultlessly by taking the ♣ A. I can stake the contract on the hearts, but I must try to do something with the diamonds first. I throw my losing clubs on the ♦AK, intending to ruff a diamond next. If either defender has Q-x-x, I can hope to draw trumps ending in dummy and pitch three hearts on the good diamonds. But on the second high diamond, the queen falls from West.

Now I'm up to 11 tricks, but with the diamonds 5-2, I still need extra tricks in hearts. If West is short in diamonds, a heart finesse through East isn't attractive. I suppose it could be right to start the hearts, but instead I take the ♠KA to see if the trumps break. Both defenders play low politely. Next I take the ♥AK, and four low hearts appear.

I don't like it. The odds are still against a 3-3 heart break, but if I let the ♥J ride, playing West for Q-9-8-3, I must also hope he has the last trump. So I lead the ♥J, and when West follows smoothly with the nine, I ruff hopefully.

Alas, East overruffs, and West still gets the ♥Q. Down two. If I pass the ♥J, I only save the second undertrick.

"He got you," my partner groans. What's he talking about? I don't know – but I do a moment later. West exposes his hand, and a low diamond is nestled there.

```
              ♠ A 7 2
              ♥ 5 2
              ♦ A K J 5 4 3
              ♣ A 3
  ♠ 9 6                        ♠ J 5 3
  ♥ Q 9 8 3                    ♥ 7 6
  ♦ Q 8 7                      ♦ 10 9 6 2
  ♣ K Q 9 4                    ♣ J 10 6 5
              ♠ K Q 10 8 4
              ♥ A K J 10 4
              ♦ —
              ♣ 8 7 2
```

West, the dog, falsecarded with the ♦Q, applying the principle of playing the card he'd soon be known to hold. If instead he plays low on the top diamonds, I'll ruff a diamond to drop the queen and easily make the slam. His falsecard offered me a losing option. I'm annoyed at myself for being taken it, but I have to admire West's play.

One risk in bidding speculative grand slams is that the other pair may not even bid six. At the other table, South opened 1♠, and North responded 2♦, a game-force in their style. When South rebid 2♥, North continued with 2♠. South then jumped to 4♠, trying to suggest a good hand with club losers, but North didn't get the message. He thought South was suggesting a dead minimum based on the "fast-arrival" principle and passed after much thought. South played hurriedly and took 11 tricks for +650. (I would be inclined to blame the 2/1 style for this result. Perhaps South's 4♠ bid was anti-systemic — depending on whose book on the system you rely on — but I see nothing illogical about it.)

So we were lucky. We lost only 13 IMPs instead of the minimum of 17 I expected. Alas, we had too many such "lucky" deals in this match.

****

As I See It

Discipline, Where Are Ye?

If bridge had been played in the Jurassic, I'd have been a brontosaurus: slow, plodding and lacking imagination. My ideas on bidding involve the quaint notion that soundness and discipline will win in the long run.

These days, players are velociraptors. It's every creature for himself in the auction, and unilateral decisions and other flights of fancy abound. This approach works for my opponents occasionally, but not for me.

In an IMP game on the net, my partner was a well known expert.

Dlr: North
Vul: None

```
              ♠ 8 4
              ♥ A 10 9 8 7
              ♦ 9 8 3
              ♣ A K 8
♠ A K 5                      ♠ 10 9 3
♥ K Q 5 4 2                  ♥ 6
♦ 10 6 2                     ♦ K Q J 7 5
♣ J 4                        ♣ Q 7 5 2
              ♠ Q J 7 6 2
              ♥ J 3
              ♦ A 4
              ♣ 10 9 6 3
```

WEST	NORTH	EAST	SOUTH
	1♥	3♦(!)	Dbl
Pass	Pass(!)	Pass	

37

East's 3♦ wouldn't have occurred to me (I hope). This is a "one-man army" bid, used by players who heard bridge is a partnership game but dismissed it as a rumor. A preempt should be descriptive as well as obstructive; otherwise, how can your partner tell when to save, compete or double? Jump to 3♦ on East's hand and you'll be right or wrong, but your partner might as well be on Neptune.

Anyway, I scraped up a negative double, and after West passed, my partner huddled ... and passed.

I led the ♥J: queen, ace. My partner cashed the ♣ K so I could signal low if my ♥J had been singleton. Since it hadn't, I played the ten, and North then took the ♣ A and led a heart. Declarer threw a spade, won in dummy and led a trump to my ace. I returned a club, but he ruffed in dummy, took the ♠AK, ruffed a spade, drew trumps and claimed.

A precise defense beats 3♦. I must start with ace and a low trump. Declarer wins in dummy and leads a low club. North wins and shifts to the ♠8: nine, jack, king. Another club goes to North's ace, and he leads his last trump. Declarer tries a heart to the queen and ace, and North then leads another spade. Since I hold the ♠7, East must lose a club or a spade in the end.

After I led the ♥J, we were done for. We can stop a club ruff in dummy or lead spades twice to break up the impending black-suit squeeze against me, but we can't do both.

I suppose I might have led a trump; but North's pass to 3♦ doubled without trump tricks was asking for trouble. A disciplined player takes out takeout doubles; the disciplined call with North's hand was 3♥.

Everyone would pass, and the play would go well despite the 5-1 trump break. North would take the ♦K with the ace and return a diamond. East would win and shift to a trump, ducked to North's seven. North ruffs a diamond, cashes the ♣ AK and exits with a club. The defense takes their two spades, but North ruffs the next spade and leads a low trump, forcing West to lead a trump into the A-10 at the end. Down one. Double-dummy defense, with East leading a trump and West playing an honor(!), would result in down two.

Minus 50 would have been an acceptable result on our cards. Minus 470 wasn't.

Long-term Effects

IMPs, East-West vulnerable. As West you hold

♠ K 8
♥ 5
♦ Q J 8 7 4
♣ Q 10 9 8 5

WEST	NORTH	EAST	SOUTH
	1♥	1♠	Dbl
?			

What is your call?

Unlucky Louie (a member of the imaginary club in my syndicated column) told me that he and his wife had caught their teenage daughter fooling around with an electrical outlet.

"Obviously," I said, "she needs to be grounded."

Many of today's teenagers live for the moment, with little concern for the long-term consequences of their actions. Many bridge players have never grown up: they forget that although a bid may be safe temporarily, the auction doesn't end until there are three successive passes.

I watched the deal below in a strong IMP game:

Dlr: North
Vul: E-W

```
                    ♠ 6 3 2
                    ♥ K J 9 6 3 2
                    ♦ A 2
                    ♣ A 4
    ♠ K 8                           ♠ A Q 10 7 4
    ♥ 5                             ♥ A 10 7 4
    ♦ Q J 8 7 4                     ♦ K 6
    ♣ Q 10 9 8 5                    ♣ 3 2
                    ♠ J 9 5
                    ♥ Q 8
                    ♦ 10 9 5 3
                    ♣ K J 7 6
```

WEST	NORTH	EAST	SOUTH
	1♥	1♠	Dbl
2♠	3♥	3♠	All Pass

Presumably, West raised to 2♠ because he thought East could make it or at least would have a play for it. The snag was that the auction rolled on. When North competed with 3♥ on his six-card suit, East had to judge. Perhaps at IMPs East should have passed since he had a promising defensive hand, but he visualized a singleton heart in dummy, hence a few heart ruffs, and took the push to 3♠.

South led the ♥Q. Facing an unexpected and disappointing dummy, East took the ♥A and led the ♦K, winning when South signalled with the five. A second diamond went to the queen and ace, and North then shifted to a trump, making declarer's task impossible.*

I didn't care for West's 2♠ bid. I thought it was a partner-trapping and losing action. (Advocates of the Law of Total Tricks might say that it fouled up East's LOTT evaluation.) I suppose a "Snapdragon" double, showing clubs plus spade tolerance, was possible, but if West prefers a disciplined pass, North will rebid 2♥. After two passes, West is entitled to back in with 2♠, but then if North-South compete to 3♥, East will pass and East-West will probably be +100.

Principle: consider an action's long-term consequences.

----

*Oh, all right. I cannot tell a lie. In real life, East made 3♠. He took the ♥A and led the ♦K, and North took his ace immediately, cashed the ♣A and led another club. South took the king and led a second heart. Declarer ruffed in dummy and led the ♣Q, ruffed by North and overruffed. Declarer next went to the ♦Q and led the ♦J, ruffed and overruffed again. He ruffed a heart with the ♠K, ruffed a diamond for his seventh trick and still had the ♠AQ for nine tricks.

If you knew your opponents would misdefend, you could always misbid. But it's better to earn good results with sound bidding judgment than to depend on your opponents to blow a straightforward defense.

Hoaxed

The greatest fraud ever perpetrated on the public, with the possible exception of Piltdown Man, is "eight ever, nine never." Consider the clubs in the deal below. "Nine never" tells you to play for the drop of the queen; but with fewer cards, to finesse against the opponent of choice would be correct.

Many players know this "rule" has a tenuous mathematical basis. Even with nine cards, a finesse is scarcely inferior. With even a shadow of a clue from the bidding or play, declarers should ignore "nine never" and back their judgment; and on many deals, factors such as timing, avoidance or control may influence declarer's play.

```
Dlr: East          ♠ 9 5 2
Vul: N-S           ♥ Q 6
IMPs               ♦ A Q 6 2
                   ♣ A 10 7 3
     ♠ J 8 3                      ♠ A 10 7 6 4
     ♥ 10 8 2                     ♥ K J 9 5 4
     ♦ J 10 7 4                   ♦ 9 3
     ♣ Q 8 4                      ♣ 6
                   ♠ K Q
                   ♥ A 7 3
                   ♦ K 8 5
                   ♣ K J 9 5 2
```

WEST	NORTH	EAST	SOUTH
		Pass	1NT
Pass	3NT	All Pass	

Almost every West led the ♦4. At the table I watched, South won with the king and put his faith in "nine never." He cashed the ♣ AK. East did well to throw spades, and West won the third club and shifted to a heart. When East covered dummy's queen, South was sunk. He had only eight tricks and no time to set up a spade for one more.

A couple of Souths made the correct technical play in clubs: king, then low to the ten. Even if East had held the queen, South would have been safe. East couldn't shift to a heart without giving South a second heart trick and nine tricks in all, and if East returned a diamond, South would have time to force out the ♠A for nine tricks.

41

One South produced the play I liked best. After taking the ♦K at the first trick, he continued with the ace and queen. When East threw a spade, South knew West had started with only four diamonds. South then reasoned that if West had four cards in a major suit, he might well have led that suit after 1NT-3NT. So South placed West with at least three clubs and picked up the ♣ Q to make an overtrick.

"Nine never." Horseradish!

Bidding over Preempts

Here's a quiz. With neither side vulnerable, you hold as dealer

♠ 7 2   ♥ 5   ♦ K 9 3   ♣ A J 10 9 6 3 2.

Since you believe preempts can still be the vintage variety, you open 3♣ . The opponents stay out. What do you do next if your partner responds

(a) 3♦
(b) 3♥
(c) 3♠
(d) 3NT
(e) 4♣

I was watching what was billed as an expert IMP game when this deal appeared:

```
Dlr: North        ♠ 9 6 5
Vul: N-S          ♥ 7 2
                  ♦ 7 4
                  ♣ A K 9 7 5 3
        ♠ 4                        ♠ K 7 3 2
        ♥ A 9 8 5                  ♥ K J 6
        ♦ 9 8                      ♦ Q J 5 3 2
        ♣ Q J 10 8 4 2             ♣ 6
                  ♠ A Q J 10 8
                  ♥ Q 10 4 3
                  ♦ A K 10 6
                  ♣ —
```

42

WEST	NORTH	EAST	SOUTH
	3♣ (!)	Pass	3♠
Pass	Pass(!)	Pass	

Curmudgeon though I am, I might have opened 3♣ as West, but North's preempt was beyond the pale. Maybe he didn't notice the vulnerability. Then, when South bid 3♠, North didn't think his three trumps, two side doubletons and ♣ AK sufficed to raise.

Against 3♠, West led a high club, and South, who had done well to bid, also did well not to comment on North's actions or the dummy. South threw a heart on the ♣ A and led a heart to his ten, and West won and switched to a trump. South won with the ten, cashed the ♦AK, ruffed a diamond and led the ♣ K: ruff by East, overruff. South ruffed his last diamond and led another heart from dummy, and East took the king and led the ♦Q. South ruffed again, cashed the ♥Q and ♠A for ten tricks and lost the last trick to the ♠K.

Not even a trump opening lead would beat 4♠. North should have raised even if 3♠ wasn't forcing, but below-game new-suit responses to preempts are 100% forcing. For North to bid a new suit—even a good one—with only a fair hand would make no sense.

(Digression: About 20 years ago, a problem something like this appeared in The Bridge World. East opens 3♣, South passes, West bids 3♠, North doubles, East passes. What should South do with

♠ J 4 ♥ A J 9 7 3 ♦ Q 7 5 3 ♣ 10 4 ?

Most experts chose a 4♥ bid, but Edgar Kaplan and a few others thought North had spades. North would have other actions if he had the red suits, but how else could he combat a psychic 3♠ response by West? Luckily, psychic maneuvers over preempts are uncommon.)

Back to the quiz. With neither side vulnerable, you open 3♣ as dealer with

♠ 7 2 ♥ 5 ♦ K 9 3 ♣ A J 10 9 6 3 2.

If partner responds 3♦, bid 4♥, a splinter bid showing a diamond fit and heart shortness. You have the best possible hand in support of diamonds.

43

If he responds 3♥, bid 3NT. You'd bid 3♠ with a stopper in spades, and partner won't expect you to have stoppers in two side suits.

If he responds 3♠, raise to 4♠. If he responds 3NT, pass; he may be bluffing, but you must presume he wants to play there. If he raises to 4♣, pass; his raise is preemptive or tactical, not a try for game.

Suppose you open 3♦ on

♠ 4   ♥ J 5   ♦ A J 9 6 5 3 2   ♣ 10 8 4.

If partner responds 3♥, raise to 4♥. Your hand isn't promising enough for a 3♠ cue-bid, and anyway, your partner might interpret that bid as showing a spade trick for notrump.

If he responds 3♠, bid 4♦. This is your weakest action.

If he responds 4♣, raise to 5♣ or cue-bid 4♠.

If he jumps to 4♠, pass; he's on his own. But since a 3♠ response would have been forcing, it's possible to play a jump as an asking bid. If partner had a hand such as

♠ 9 6 2   ♥ A K Q 6 4   ♦ K 8 7   ♣ A 9

he'd need to know about your spade holding to bid 6♦.

****

At My Club

Dlr: South
Vul: Both

```
              ♠ 10 6 2
              ♥ K 10 4
              ♦ A 5 2
              ♣ 6 5 3 2
♠ K Q J 9 8 4              ♠ —
♥ 7                       ♥ 9 8 6 5 3 2
♦ J 10 6                  ♦ Q 9 8 4
♣ 10 9 8                  ♣ K J 4
              ♠ A 7 5 3
              ♥ A Q J
              ♦ K 7 3
              ♣ A Q 7
```

WEST	NORTH	EAST	SOUTH
			1♣
2♠	Pass	Pass	2NT
Pass	3NT	All Pass	

Cy the Cynic is something of an enigma at my club. Nobody knows whether he has family or money, and his former occupation, if ever he had one, is a mystery. Our efforts to pry information out of Cy have developed into a running gag.

"Cy, did you work in an underwear shop?"
"Briefly," he replies.
"Did you manage a towel factory?"
"For a while, but it folded."
"Were you a windshield repairman, Cy?"
"I tried but I couldn't get a break."

Cy got a break in this deal but didn't take advantage. As declarer at 3NT, he captured West's ♠K opening lead—to duck was pointless—led a heart to dummy and returned a club. East alertly started to unblock by following with the jack, and Cy's queen won. Cy next cashed the ♣ A, and East continued his good defense by dropping the king. Cy couldn't afford to lead another club. He judged rightly to cash his red-suit tricks and give up. Down one.

To take three club tricks and nine tricks in all, Cy needed East to hold ♣ KJx—and he got that break. How would you play the hand?

It's not easy to see, but South must cash the ♣ A at the second trick. Suppose East drops the jack. South then leads a heart to dummy and returns a club. If East plays the king, South plays low. He later cashes the queen and gets to dummy with the ♦A for the 13th club.

If instead East plays low on the second club, South takes the queen and leads a third club to East.

****

Sit Beside Me

In a home team game, I'm blessed with a partner I can trust. Only our side is vulnerable, and I hold

♠ 8 6 4 2
♥ A Q 4 2
♦ K 4
♣ 10 7 3

My partner deals and opens 1♦, I respond 1♥ and he bids 2♣. The opponents sit silently by.

To pass could miss an easy game. Partner's simple change of suit could conceal as many as 18 points. I can't try 2NT with only nine points and no sign of a spade stopper, so I take a "false preference" to 2♦. My partner wouldn't bid this way with 4-4 in the minors — he'd open 1♣ or rebid 1NT — so if he passes 2♦, we'll be at a playable spot.

Partner next bids 2♥, and I must reconsider game chances. Even at matchpoints, partner wouldn't bid 2♥ with a minimum hand. With a hand such as

♠3 ♥KJ5 ♦AQ863 ♣K965,

he'd have raised 1♥ to 2♥. I could have as few as six points for my preference; hence when he bids a third time anyway, he suggests substantial extra strength.

Since I have maximum values with all working honors, I'm worth game. I can't settle for a re-raise to 3♥ — partner might pass — and though

47

I could try a mark-time bid such as 2♠, my hearts are decent, and I won't mind playing at a 4-3 fit. I jump to 4♥, and everyone passes.

West expects dummy to have spade shortness. He leads the ♥10. Dummy is not quite what I expected.

♠ 7
♥ K 8 3
♦ A Q J 7 5 3
♣ A J 6

♠ 8 6 4 2
♥ A Q 4 2
♦ K 4
♣ 10 7 3

WEST	NORTH	EAST	SOUTH
	1♦	Pass	1♥
Pass	2♣	Pass	2♦
Pass	2♥	Pass	4♥
All Pass			

North's improvised rebid of 2♣ was unlikely to come to harm. He thought 2♣ was more flexible than a jump to 3♦. If I raised to 3♣ or bid 2NT, he'd continue with 3♦ or 3♥, forcing. painting a good picture of his distribution. If I passed 2♣, that contract might be as good as any.

I wonder if I should try for a spade ruff in dummy. I can take the ♥K, concede a spade, win the trump return, ruff a spade, come to my ♦K and try to draw trumps. If they break 4-2, I can start the diamonds, hoping to discard my other spades before the defender with the high trump can ruff. The ♣A will still be a dummy entry, and I can discard clubs on the diamonds.

That plan seems reasonable, but it's no sure thing. If diamonds break 4-1, I may lose three spades and a trump. Moreover, a club shift may be troublesome. There must be a better line. After all, I have plenty of winners and only one fast loser.

It seems to me I recall a similar situation. What was that deal from a Venice Cup? If I can just draw trumps, I'll make the contract easily!

On the ♥10, I play low from dummy—and low from my hand! West leads another trump, but now I can draw trumps with the king, ace and queen, run the diamonds and take the ♣A for ten tricks. The full deal:

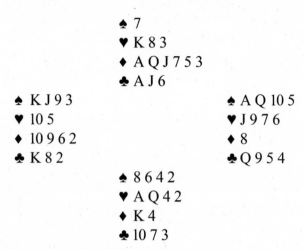

```
                    ♠ 7
                    ♥ K 8 3
                    ♦ A Q J 7 5 3
                    ♣ A J 6
      ♠ K J 9 3                      ♠ A Q 10 5
      ♥ 10 5                         ♥ J 9 7 6
      ♦ 10 9 6 2                     ♦ 8
      ♣ K 8 2                        ♣ Q 9 5 4
                    ♠ 8 6 4 2
                    ♥ A Q 4 2
                    ♦ K 4
                    ♣ 10 7 3
```

If I pursue a spade ruff in dummy, I probably go down. (If I win the first trump in dummy and lead a spade, East can prevail if he wins and continues spades. As it happens, I could make 4♥ by taking the ♥K and ♥A and starting the diamonds.)

We gained an IMP on the board. At the other table, North jumped to 3♦ over 1♥, and South shut his eyes and tried 3NT. After the defense cashed four spades, he claimed.

The Venice Cup deal I recalled was something like this:

```
                    ♠ A Q 3 2
                    ♥ 9 8 3
                    ♦ K 6 5
                    ♣ A 10 4

                    ♠ K 6 4
                    ♥ J 4
                    ♦ A 4
                    ♣ K Q 9 7 5 2
```

South became declarer at 4♠, and West cashed a high heart and switched to a diamond. South went down, missing her best line: to play a low trump from both hands at the third trick.

In a Sectional Open Pairs final, both sides are vulnerable, and I'm South, in fourth position, with

♠ 10 6 5 3
♥ A Q 9 5 4
♦ K J
♣ K 6

I hear three passes and open 1♥. This is a good opening bid in any position, with decent defensive values and length in both majors. After a pass at my left, my partner jumps to 3♣, and right-hand opponent passes.

My opening bid must have improved partner's hand, otherwise he'd have no reason to jump and crowd our auction. I expect good heart support and club values. My ♣K is a valuable card, I have decent trumps and partner's hand may be short in spades. I take the pressure off with a jump to 4♥, and everyone passes.

West leads the ♠A, and partner puts down a promising dummy.

♠ K 7
♥ J 10 6 2
♦ 8 6
♣ A Q 7 4 2

♠ 10 6 5 3
♥ A Q 9 5 4
♦ K J
♣ K 6

WEST	NORTH	EAST	SOUTH
Pass	Pass	Pass	1♥
Pass	3♣	Pass	4♥
All Pass			

West continues with the ♠4, and East drops the queen under dummy's king. Since it's matchpoints, I mustn't leave any overtricks on the table. At the third trick I let the ♥J ride. West produces the king, alas, and leads a third spade. I have to ruff that with the ♥10, and sure enough, East discards a diamond.

When I lead another trump to my ace, West discards. Wonderful. If trumps had split 2-2, I almost certainly could have made an overtrick by cashing the ♣AKQ for one diamond discard, ruffing a club if necessary, ruffing my last spade in dummy and pitching my last diamond on the good fifth club. (I might have been better off by starting with a low trump to my queen, but that wasn't obvious.)

As it is, I draw trumps and try the top clubs, discarding my last spade. West discards, so I must guess the diamonds to make the contract. Fortunately, the winning play is clear: West, a passed hand, has shown the ♠AJ842 and ♥K, so the ♦A lies with East. A diamond to the king wins, and I am +620. The full deal:

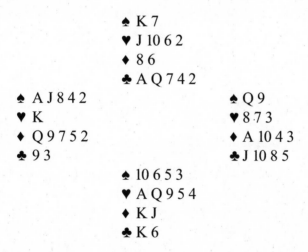

```
              ♠ K 7
              ♥ J 10 6 2
              ♦ 8 6
              ♣ A Q 7 4 2
♠ A J 8 4 2                    ♠ Q 9
♥ K                           ♥ 8 7 3
♦ Q 9 7 5 2                   ♦ A 10 4 3
♣ 9 3                         ♣ J 10 8 5
              ♠ 10 6 5 3
              ♥ A Q 9 5 4
              ♦ K J
              ♣ K 6
```

West seems to have overreacted to the vulnerability when he never took any action.

Many Norths would have jumped to 3♥ over 1♥, but the value-showing 3♣ was more descriptive and cost nothing. Suppose my hand had been J653,AQ954,KJ4,3. Then I'd have signed off at 3♥, and though 4♥ might make, I wouldn't regret playing at a partscore. But if North jumped to 3♦ with a hand such as 84,J1062,A10973,A6, I'd be happy to bid 4♥.

In a Sectional Swiss Teams, we're up against a team we need to beat to have a chance for first place. Neither side is vulnerable, and as West I hold

♠ A 6 3 2
♥ 5
♦ K J 10 9 8
♣ J 5 2

North passes as dealer, East opens 1♥ and South overcalls 1♠.

I have enough values to act but no ideal action. My hand isn't strong enough to bid 2♦, and a 1NT bid would suggest at least a doubleton heart. Many experts would make a negative double, but I'm not eager to hear my partner bid clubs or rebid hearts. I am content to pass. If North also passes, my partner will reopen if his hand is short in spades, as seems likely.

Instead, North jumps to 2NT, natural and invitational. East passes and South tries 3♣. I pass again, and North takes a 3♠ preference, passed to me. I expect we can beat this, but I'm not confident enough to double for an extra 50 points at the risk of being -530.

Against 3♠ undoubled I lead my singleton heart, and dummy is about as I expect.

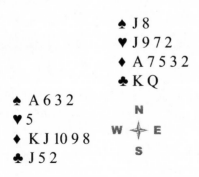

                    ♠ J 8
                    ♥ J 9 7 2
                    ♦ A 7 5 3 2
                    ♣ K Q
    ♠ A 6 3 2
    ♥ 5   N
    ♦ K J 10 9 8   W + E
    ♣ J 5 2   S

WEST	NORTH	EAST	SOUTH
	Pass	1♥	1♠
Pass	2NT	Pass	3♣
Pass	3♠	All Pass	

South calls for the ♥9, and East wins with the ten and leads the ace. South ruffs with the ♠4, and I overruff with the six. South looks surprised.

I'm surprised also. East's hearts were A-K-Q-10-6-4-3, and he can't have much outside. I wonder why he didn't preempt. Maybe he thought he had less reason to do so after North passed.

East's lead of the ♥A looks like a suit-preference signal for diamonds, so I return the ♦K. Dummy's ace wins, and East drops the queen. South cashes the ♣KQ and leads the ♠8: nine, ten, ace. I cash the ♦J, but declarer ruffs the next diamond, draws my last two trumps and puts down the ♣A. My jack falls, and he claims the last two tricks with good clubs. We are -140, and I'm glad I didn't double. The full deal:

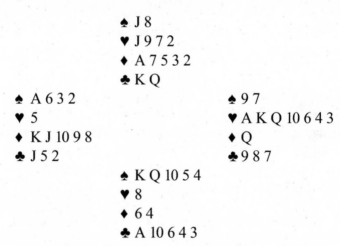

```
                        ♠ J 8
                        ♥ J 9 7 2
                        ♦ A 7 5 3 2
                        ♣ K Q
      ♠ A 6 3 2                      ♠ 9 7
      ♥ 5                            ♥ A K Q 10 6 4 3
      ♦ K J 10 9 8                   ♦ Q
      ♣ J 5 2                        ♣ 9 8 7
                        ♠ K Q 10 5 4
                        ♥ 8
                        ♦ 6 4
                        ♣ A 10 6 4 3
```

At the other table, East opened 1♥ again, but my teammate sitting South tried 2♥, a Michaels cue-bid showing length in spades and a minor suit. After West passed, North bid 2NT, asking South to bid his minor. North planned to bid 3♠ next, hoping South would interpret his sequence as a try for game. Since 2NT was conventional, East was willing to compete with 3♥; at my table, East passed 2NT because it promised hearts. Since North hoped for a plus on defense, he sold out.

South led the ♠K, ducked, and another spade. East won and led a trump to his ten, playing South for a singleton heart on the bidding since South hadn't led or shifted to a singleton diamond. East then drew trumps and led the ♦Q, and the defense was helpless. North could win and cash two clubs but then had to lead to dummy, and East's last club went away.

We lost 7 IMPs, and I realized only later that I could have saved part of the loss. When declarer has a two-suited hand, best defense is often to threaten him with the loss of trump control so he can't win tricks in his second suit. Instead of overruffing with my ♠6 at the second trick, I should have thrown a diamond!

South can take the ♣KQ and start the trumps, and I win the second trump and lead the ♦K to dummy's ace. South must ruff something to get back to his hand, and I have more trumps than he does. He can take only eight tricks. It's not easy to see, but South could always make 3♠ by pitching a diamond on the second heart instead of ruffing.

As for the bidding at my table—specifically, my pass over 1♠—it seems to me that players often feel compelled to act even though they have no good action. I am never reluctant to pass and wait when no bid is perfectly descriptive.

Near the end of a one-session Masters Pairs, I estimate our score as average. We've been unlucky, of course. Our opponents have played much better than we have, and nothing is unluckier than that. On the first board of the round, our opponents took 16 bids and most of the 15 minutes to reach a laydown slam. On the second board, I pick up

♠ Q J 9 7 6 3 2
♥ 8
♦ A Q J 5 4
♣ —

I'm South. West, the dealer, passes, and my partner opens 1NT, promising 16 to 18 points.

The time clock is ticking, and we still have some rounds to play. I'd also like to provide a startling contrast to the first board, so I bash into 6♠.

I don't think this action is terribly swingy. I'll have a play for 12 tricks most of the time, especially if I give the opening leader no help. Still, if my partner puts down a dummy such as 85,KQ53,K83,AKQ2 (a gruesome thought!), I'll feel bad because I'll have handed the opponents a top with a bid some players might consider frivolous.

Everyone passes to 6♠, and West leads the ♥K. I love that lead. Before I even see dummy, I'm sure I'll make this slam. North has either the ♥A or at most the queen, and either way, he'll have suitable values.

```
            ♠ A 5 4
            ♥ A 6 3
            ♦ K 7 2
            ♣ K Q 8 4

            ♠ Q J 9 7 6 3 2
            ♥ 8
            ♦ A Q J 5 4
            ♣ —
```

WEST	NORTH	EAST	SOUTH
Pass	1NT	Pass	6♠
All Pass			

His club honors are wasted, but 6♠ is all but cold. In fact, I expect many pairs to reach slam, so I may need an overtrick to score well.

I take the ♥A and am about to ruff a heart to finesse in trumps when it occurs to me that I might get some helpful information. At the second trick I call for the ♣K. East plays low without a tremor, and I ruff. Now I can place West with the ♣A as well as the ♥KQ, but he didn't open the bidding. I'm sure East has the ♠K.

At the third trick I lead a trump to the ace. If West has the guarded king, and East has been good enough to duck with the ♣A, I'll pay off. As it happens, the singleton king falls from East, and I draw the last trump and claim 13 tricks. The full deal:

```
                    ♠ A 5 4
                    ♥ A 6 3
                    ♦ K 7 2
                    ♣ K Q 8 4
    ♠ 10 8                          ♠ K
    ♥ K Q 10 4                      ♥ J 9 7 5 2
    ♦ 10 6                          ♦ 9 8 3
    ♣ A 9 6 3 2                     ♣ J 10 7 5
                    ♠ Q J 9 7 6 3 2
                    ♥ 8
                    ♦ A Q J 5 4
                    ♣ —
```

My lead of the ♣K was a "discovery play": an active attempt to get information. The opportunity for such plays knocks more often than players imagine.

As for the bidding, I fear my leap to slam was wrong. A "bash" that keeps the opponents in the dark works occasionally, but the best approach in the long run is "Bash into games, investigate for slams."

Next time I'll look for slam intelligently: I could respond 2♥, a transfer to spades, and jump to 4♦ next as a slam try. If North signed off at 4♠, I'd trust him and pass. On the actual deal, he'd cue-bid 4♥, and I could bid 6♠ with confidence.

****

As I See It

You Be the Judge (and Jury)

"I'd have asked for a trial by jury, but I'd have been putting my fate in the hands of 12 people who weren't even smart enough to get out of jury duty." – Cy the Cynic, after paying a fine for a traffic violation.

A feature of most bridge magazines — and a popular pastime among players — is apportioning the blame for disasters. You can be the judge and jury on the layout below, where it's safe to assume somebody did something wrong: North-South lost 800 points on a partscore deal. The scene was an all-expert IMP game on the internet with more than 100 kibitzers.

```
Dlr: North        ♠ A 10 9 8
Vul: N-S          ♥ Q J 3
                  ♦ 5
                  ♣ A Q J 8 2
    ♠ J 6 2                    ♠ K 7 5
    ♥ K 10 9 7 5 4             ♥ 6
    ♦ A J 4                    ♦ Q 10 9 3 2
    ♣ 3                        ♣ K 10 6 4
                  ♠ Q 4 3
                  ♥ A 8 2
                  ♦ K 8 7 6
                  ♣ 9 7 5
```

WEST	NORTH	EAST	SOUTH
	1♣	Pass	1NT
2♥	3♣	Pass	3♥
Pass	3♠	Pass	3NT
Pass	Pass	Dbl	All Pass

West led the ♥7. (Some of the kibitzers wondered if East's double of 3NT asked for a club opening lead. It didn't. After North rebid clubs, the double suggested club strength but directed no particular lead. East simply said 3NT would fail.)

South put up dummy's queen, winning, and led the ♣A and ♣Q. East ducked, and South continued with the ♣8. When East played low, South mis-guessed by letting the eight ride. Perhaps he hoped East had the ♦A and, therefore, West had the ♣K; but West took the ♣J and returned a spade. When South finessed, East won and shifted to the ♦10. The result was down three. 3♣ might have gone peacefully down one undoubled for -100.

Who was to blame for the disaster (aside from East, who doubled 3NT and earned himself a big, fat profit)? The kibitzers had their opinions. Some thought North's 3♣ was at fault; others heaped scorn on South's 3♥ cue-bid.

My view: North's bid of 3♣ was questionable; South's failure to pass it when he had limited his strength, more or less, was a felony. North's 3♣ was strictly competitive, and when South bid again, it meant that North had a choice of defending 2♥ or playing at game.

I think South should have passed 3♣ without looking at his hand. What do you think?

A Bidding Principle

At IMPs, neither side vulnerable, you hold as North

♠ Q J 8 5 3
♥ 8 7 2
♦ Q
♣ J 9 8 7

WEST	NORTH	EAST	SOUTH
	Pass	Pass	2♣
Pass	2♦	3♥	4♣
Pass	?		

What is your call?

If I were asked what principle good bidders adhere to most closely, I might reply that they seldom neglect to show support for their partner's suit. Suppose you hold

♠ A 7 5
♥ Q 10 5
♦ Q J 9 4
♣ A K 5

You open 1NT, and your partner responds 3♠, natural and forcing. A mastermind bids 3NT because of his balanced pattern; a disciplined player raises to 4♠ – what his partner wants him to do with three-card support.

♠ A Q 7
♥ K 7 5
♦ A K 6 5
♣ K 7 3

You open 1♦, your partner responds 1♠, you jump to 2NT and he tries 3♥. To show the spade support again is correct, but since partner has promised five or more spades, your values are slammish and your support is excellent, jump to 4♠.

♠ 8
♥ K J 5
♦ A Q 6 4 3
♣ Q 10 6 4

You open 1♦, and partner responds 1♥. Raise to 2♥. Auctions are easier when a trump suit is set quickly. If instead you rebid 2♣ and partner returns to 2♦, jumps to 3♦ (invitational) or bids 2NT, your hand won't be strong enough to bid again, and you may miss a heart fit. Moreover, the opponents may be about to compete in spades, and unless you support the hearts now, you may never have a convenient chance.

When I watched the deal below, North-South missed a laydown grand slam and conducted a contentious post-mortem.

Dlr: North
Vul: None

```
                    ♠ Q J 8 5 3
                    ♥ 8 7 2
                    ♦ Q
                    ♣ J 9 8 7
   ♠ 10 9                             ♠ 7 6 4 2
   ♥ A K 10 6                         ♥ Q J 9 5 4 3
   ♦ 10 9 8 7 5 2                     ♦ 3
   ♣ 10                              ♣ 5 2
                    ♠ A K
                    ♥ —
                    ♦ A K J 6 4
                    ♣ A K Q 6 4 3
```

Many North-Souths reached 7♣. At some tables they had a smooth ride when East-West stayed out of the auction:

NORTH	SOUTH
Pass	2♣
2♦	3♣
4♣/5♣	7♣

Other North-Souths achieved odd results. At three tables the contract was 6♠ by North, making when East led his singleton diamond. Three North-Souths halted at 5♣ on auctions you don't want to know about. One West pulled off a "striped-tail ape" double of 6♣. North-South neglected to redouble and scored only +1190, but they still gained heavily against par since a few East-Wests saved at 7♥ for -800.

North-Souths who stopped at 6♣ usually had to contend with interference. East often bid hearts, and at some tables West jacked up the auction up to 6♥ right away. When West displayed less enterprise, North-South often reached 7♣ and were usually allowed to play there.

This was the auction at the table I watched:

WEST	NORTH	EAST	SOUTH
	Pass	Pass	2♣
Pass	2♦	3♥	4♣
Pass(!)	4♠	Pass	5♦
Pass	6♣	Pass	Pass
Pass(!)			

The bid that triggered the discussion after South claimed 13 tricks was North's 4♠.

South: "You had good club support. Why didn't you raise?"

North: "Because I'm not a genius. You could have had a spade fit and a more balanced hand. How can we get to spades if I don't bid them? You had all the controls, including a heart control."

North's argument left me cold. In a crowded slam auction at IMPs, North's duty was to confirm a fit. If he had raised to 5♣, South might have tried 7♣. But as North actually bid, he could have held

♠ J 9 6 4 3 2
♥ 8 7 6
♦ 8 7
♣ 8 7

When in doubt, raise. But you should seldom be in doubt.

Lead-Directing Bids

IMPs, both sides vulnerable. As North you hold

♠ J 3
♥ Q J 8 6 5 4
♦ 10 9 6 4
♣ 7

WEST	NORTH	EAST	SOUTH
		1♠	2♥
2♠	?		

What is your call?

Some deals find a permanent niche in a player's memory. In January 1981 I was playing in a Knockout Teams semifinal at a Nashville Regional, and halfway through the second half, with neither side vulnerable, I picked up as South

♠ 8 6 4
♥ 4
♦ 10 8 6 4 2
♣ A Q 7 3

WEST	NORTH	EAST	SOUTH
	Pass	Pass	Pass
1♥	1♠	2♣	?

I tried 3♣, and the effect was enchanting. The opponents bid to 4♥, but my partner led the ♣K from K-x. Dummy had J-x-x-x, and four rounds of clubs gave declarer a problem in trumps he failed to solve: my partner scored a trick with his J-x-x.

Opportunities for lead-directing bids don't arise often, but such bids can gain hundreds of points. In a textbook example, East-West are vulnerable:

WEST	NORTH	EAST	SOUTH
1♠	3♦	4♦	?

♠ A 7 4
♥ 9 8 6 4 2
♦ K Q 7 5
♣ 4

South has an obvious sacrifice at 5♦, but to set up a defense against 5♠ if East-West push on, South bids 5♣. In the best of all worlds, North leads a club against 5♠, and when South takes the ♠A, he puts North in with a diamond and gets a club ruff for down one.

In that situation, North has preempted, and South need not worry that North will commit an indiscretion such as bidding 6♣ over 5♠. But in other auctions South may have a complex tactical problem. In The Bridge

World's Master Solvers' Club (October 1991), South had to choose an action with

$$\spadesuit\ 7\ 6\ 5\ 4$$
$$\heartsuit\ J\ 9\ 7\ 6\ 4$$
$$\diamondsuit\ 5\ 4\ 3\ 2$$
$$\clubsuit\ —$$

after

WEST	NORTH	EAST	SOUTH
			Pass
1♠	2♥	2♠	?

More than half the panel bid some number of clubs, intending to direct a lead against an eventual East-West spade contract. But here, as several panelists noted, North may have a strong hand. If South bids clubs, North may misjudge, thinking South has length and strength in clubs. A reasonable plan is to jump to 4♥, preemptive. Then if East-West go to 4♠, South bids 5♣ for the lead.

I was watching an internet IMP game when North faced the problem I gave you.

Dlr: East
Vul: Both

```
                    ♠ J 3
                    ♥ Q J 8 6 5 4
                    ♦ 10 9 6 4
                    ♣ 7
    ♠ 8 6 4                         ♠ A K Q 7 2
    ♥ K                             ♥ 3
    ♦ Q 8 7 3                       ♦ K 5 2
    ♣ K 6 5 4 2                     ♣ Q J 10 9
                    ♠ 10 9 5
                    ♥ A 10 9 7 2
                    ♦ A J
                    ♣ A 8 3
```

WEST	NORTH	EAST	SOUTH
		1♠	2♥
2♠	3♣(!)	3♠	Pass
Pass	Pass(!)		

North's lead-directing 3♣ seemed to him like a good idea at the time. Indeed, East-West would be held to eight tricks at spades if North got a couple of club ruffs. But when the auction continued with a competitive 3♠ bid by East and two passes, North perversely sold out, forgetting that he had set up a defense against 4♠ and that the auction marked South with a good hand.

In fact, North's decision lost against par: South could have made 4♥ for +620, off two spades and a diamond, and North-South could have collected +500 against 4♠ doubled.

North's winning action was to raise to 4♥. If East-West bid 4♠, South might double and lead the ♥A, and North could follow with the four. If South trusted his partner, he would shift to the ♣A and a low club, get back in with the ♦A and give North a second ruff.

How did the defense go against the actual 3♠? It didn't. South, unsure what was happening, led a trump for -170.

****

At My Club

Dlr: South
Vul: Both

	♠ A 10 6 5 4	
	♥ Q 9 3	
	♦ A K Q	
	♣ J 3	

♠ K 8		♠ Q J 9 2
♥ 8 7 2		♥ K J 10 6
♦ 9 7 6 4 3 2		♦ J 10 8
♣ 8 6		♣ A 2

	♠ 7 3	
	♥ A 5 4	
	♦ 5	
	♣ K Q 10 9 7 5 4	

WEST	NORTH	EAST	SOUTH
			3♣
Pass	3♠	Pass	3NT
All Pass			

"It's been like this since the Garden of Eden," Cy the Cynic said to me at the club one day. "God told Adam that a good woman costs an arm and a leg, and Adam asked, 'What can I get for a rib?'"

Cy had partnered Wendy, my club's feminist, in a penny Chicago game. Cy is a chauvinist who believes women can barely follow suit; Wendy thinks all men are idiots and Cy is their king. The two are relentless adversaries.

"What would you lead against 3NT?" Cy asked me, giving me the West hand and the bidding.

"With such a weak hand," I said, "I suppose I'd try a heart, hoping to find East with heart length plus an entry."

"That's what I led," Cy said. He displayed the full deal.

South covered the ♥8 with dummy's nine, and Wendy, East, played the ten. Since South needed the ♥A as an entry to the clubs, he ducked. Wendy then declined to lead from her ♥K; she shifted to the ♠Q.

South took dummy's ace and led the ♣J and another club. Wendy took her ace and led a spade to Cy's king. When Cy led another heart, South claimed. Making four.

"You could have ribbed Wendy, so to speak, about her defense," I said. "She missed a 'Merrimac Coup.' If she leads the ♥K at trick two, she kills declarer's entry to the clubs, and he goes down."

"She probably thought that leading a man — the ♥K — would never accomplish anything," Cy grumbled, "whereas leading a woman — the ♠Q — was a sure thing."

PART the THIRD

Sit Beside Me

I'm playing in a home team game, and we're rotating partners for each segment. My partner for this deal is our team's weakest player—but the most enthusiastic. With both sides vulnerable, I'm in second seat as South with

    ♠ A J 10 6
    ♥ K 4
    ♦ A J 6 3
    ♣ 9 5 4

After a pass by East, I open 1♦, and my partner responds 2♣. East comes in with 2♥.

I really ought to pass. I'm old-fashioned enough to believe that free bids mean something. When you've opened on a flat 13 points with the dreaded three low cards in your partner's long suit, a pass is a fine way to slow things down. But my ♥K seems to be upgraded, and I can get my spade suit mentioned cheaply. I try 2♠, hoping I won't open a worm can.

West competes gently with 3♥, and my partner launches out into 4NT, Blackwood.

What have I done? I can't be a mastermind now. I dutifully answer 5♥, and partner bids 6♦, passed out. West leads the ♥A.

♠ Q 2
♥ 5
♦ K 9 7 5 2
♣ A Q 7 6 3

♠ A J 10 6
♥ K 4
♦ A J 6 3
♣ 9 5 4

WEST	NORTH	EAST	SOUTH
		Pass	1♦
Pass	2♣	2♥	2♠
3♥	4NT	Pass	5♥
Pass	6♦	All Pass	

North couldn't find a direct diamond raise that was appropriate, hence his temporizing 2♣ response. His 4NT was too aggressive, but this terrible slam is more my fault. If I'd had a reasonable excuse for bidding 2♠ freely — if I held, for example, AKJx,xxx,AQxxx,x — 6♦ would be cold.

I thank my partner for his dummy. Meanwhile, West shifts to the ♣2.

This looks grim. I finesse with the ♣Q, and East plays the ten. I'm not dead yet, just barely breathing. Do I have any chance? I need to pick up the trumps and win the spade finesse, but that's still only 11 tricks: five trumps, three spades, a heart and two clubs. The 12th trick must come from a squeeze.

West seems to have length in clubs. If I'm to squeeze him in spades and clubs, he must have at least four spades as well. East should have no more than six hearts on the bidding; he'd have opened 3♥ with a seven-card suit, and West might have bid more with five-card heart support. If I give West length in spades and clubs plus four hearts, I must assume East has length in diamonds. (East could be 3-6-2-2, I suppose, but I think he's more likely to have a shapely hand to bid at the two level. West might have bid 4♥ instead of 3♥ with 4-4-1-4 shape, but maybe the vulnerability deterred him.)

I take the ♦K and lead to the ♦J. West discards a heart. After taking the ♦A, I cash the ♥K and run the trumps, leaving:

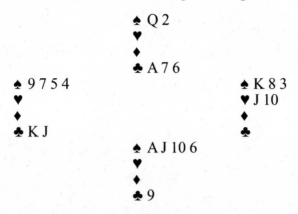

```
                    ♠ Q 2
                    ♥
                    ♦
                    ♣ A 7 6
  ♠ 9 7 5 4                          ♠ K 8 3
  ♥                                  ♥ J 10
  ♦                                  ♦
  ♣ K J                              ♣
                    ♠ A J 10 6
                    ♥
                    ♦
                    ♣ 9
```

West, still to discard, can turn in his sword. The full deal:

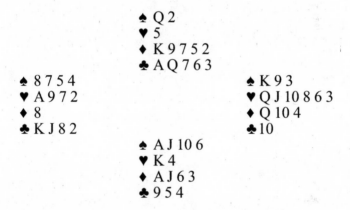

```
                    ♠ Q 2
                    ♥ 5
                    ♦ K 9 7 5 2
                    ♣ A Q 7 6 3
  ♠ 8 7 5 4                          ♠ K 9 3
  ♥ A 9 7 2                          ♥ Q J 10 8 6 3
  ♦ 8                                ♦ Q 10 4
  ♣ K J 8 2                          ♣ 10
                    ♠ A J 10 6
                    ♥ K 4
                    ♦ A J 6 3
                    ♣ 9 5 4
```

East must have wanted the classic x,KQJxxx,Kxx,xxx to open a weak 2♥.

I'm playing IMPs for fun on OKbridge, the internet site, and I am dealt the type of hand referred to as a "giraffe:

```
                    ♠ J 9 5 2
                    ♥ —
                    ♦ Q 9
                    ♣ A K 10 9 8 5 3
```

Both sides are vulnerable. West, at my left, deals and passes, and North, my partner, opens 1♥.

71

I know some players — good ones — who are so constrained by system that they'd respond 1♠ on my hand, but my notions about bidding involve giving partner a description of my hand: I bid 2♣. If North rebids 2♠, I'll bid 3♣; if he rebids 2NT, which shows a balanced minimum in our style, game may be cold, and I'll have to raise to 3NT or jump to 4♣. But if North rebids 2♥ or 2♦, I'll settle for 3♣, suggesting a moderate hand with long clubs. Since I have a seventh club, this sequence is timid, but the void in hearts is a discouraging feature.

North rebids 2♦, and I follow through with 3♣. If he passes with 104,AJ1052,AJ64,Q4, we'll miss 3NT and I'll apologize, but he may have a better hand such as K74,AK952,A874,4 where no game is odds-on.

North next bids 3♠. What's that? If he really has spades, I should raise. But he must have extra strength, and with 4-5-4-0 pattern, he might have bid 2♠ at his second turn. Does he have, say, A-x in spades or a partial stopper such as Q-x? Or does he lack any sign of a spade stopper and want me to bid 3NT if I have one?

I don't know. I'll find out when I see dummy, but I think it's unlikely he has four spades. I hate to bid 3NT with my giraffe, but it may be the right spot. Besides, I'm a believer in Hamman's Rule: "If several bids are possible, and 3NT is one of them ..."

Over my 3NT, North bids 4♣. It seems his 3♠ was an "advance cue-bid," promising club support and a spade control. Now my hand looks better. North doesn't know I have seven good clubs, first-round heart control, a working ♦Q and only a wasted jack in spades. I could bid 5♣ and leave it to him, but I think 6♣ is the value bid on my cards.

Everyone passes, and West leads the ♣6.

> ♠ A K
> ♥ A K J 10 2
> ♦ A J 7 6
> ♣ 6 4
>
> ♠ J 9 5 2
> ♥ —
> ♦ Q 9
> ♣ A K 10 9 8 5 3

WEST	NORTH	EAST	SOUTH
Pass	1♥	Pass	2♣
Pass	2♦	Pass	3♣
Pass	3♠	Pass	3NT
Pass	4♣	Pass	6♣
All Pass			

Dummy wins, and East plays the seven.

This may not be easy. There must be a winning line; I just need to find it. One brain-saving line is to take the ♣AK. If trumps break 2-2, I'll lead the ♦Q, planning to take the ace if West ducks. I can throw a diamond and a spade on the ♥AK and lead the ♥J for a ruffing finesse. Twelve tricks would be certain, and I'd still have a chance if there was a trump loser.

Suppose when I come to the ♣A, an honor drops at my left. Chances are it will be a singleton (unless West finds a subtle falsecard with Q-J-x), so I can lead the ♦Q next, take the ♦A if West doesn't cover, pitch my last diamond on a high heart, finesse in trumps and maybe lose a spade.

What about ruffing a spade in dummy? That may be best. If a defender overruffs, I can still expect seven trump tricks, two hearts, two spades and a diamond.

Figuring out all the percentages at the table is beyond me. I decide to try for the spade ruff and am about to click on the ♠K when it occurs to me to wonder about a 4-0 trump break. That's a 10% chance. I'm not sure I can do anything about it, but I can shorten my trumps by ruffing a heart at the second trick. I lead a spade next: three, king, ten; and when I return a trump from dummy, East shows out. Goodness!

I'm not down yet. I take the ♣A and ruff a spade. West follows, and the queen falls from East. I ruff another heart and cash the ♠J. The position:

```
        ♠
        ♥ A K J
        ♦ A J 7
        ♣

        ♠
        ♥
        ♦ Q 9
        ♣ K 10 9 8
```

West was 4-4 in the black suits. If he has ♦Kxx and no more hearts, I need to finesse in diamonds, then cash the ♦A and ruff a diamond. But it doesn't seem right to play West for the ♦K as well as for a specific distribution. I lead the ♦Q but take the ace when West plays low. I discard a diamond on the ♥A, and West follows.

Now I'm safe unless West was 4-4-1-4, and then the opening lead probably would have been a diamond. I ruff a diamond, and West follows. My last three cards are the ♣K109, and I can lead the ten to endplay West in trumps:

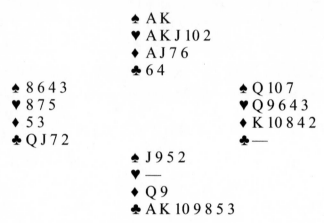

        ♠ A K
        ♥ A K J 10 2
        ♦ A J 7 6
        ♣ 6 4

♠ 8 6 4 3   ♠ Q 10 7
♥ 8 7 5   ♥ Q 9 6 4 3
♦ 5 3   ♦ K 10 8 4 2
♣ Q J 7 2   ♣ —

        ♠ J 9 5 2
        ♥ —
        ♦ Q 9
        ♣ A K 10 9 8 5 3

As the cards lay, I could have survived even if I hadn't ruffed a heart early.

One useful feature of OKbridge is that I can see what happened when other players faced this deal. Many of the auctions misfired. One top-flight North-South bid 1♥-1♠, 3♦-3NT, Pass. South never mentioned her clubs. Another North-South was playing a 2/1 response as forcing to the moon, and the bidding was 1♥-1NT(!), 3NT.

I found it annoying that these pairs gained IMPs! 3NT made, while the good 6♣ went down at many tables.

In an Open Pairs, I'm the dealer with

        ♠ K Q 10 6 4
        ♥ K 4
        ♦ K J 3
        ♣ A 5 2

It's the eternal question: 1NT or 1♠? I don't mind suppressing a five-card major to give partner an overall description of my hand with one bid. If I opened 1NT, I'd avoid the mild rebid problems if partner responded with two of a new suit to 1♠. (In our style, a 2NT rebid wouldn't promise extra strength.)

Nevertheless, I see reasons to open 1♠. Most of my values are prime and better for a suit contract. I have a heart doubleton: if I open 1NT, I may get transferred into hearts on a 5-2 fit when we have a 5-3 spade fit. My spade suit is fair, but I may need time to establish it—time I might not have at notrump. I'd be more willing to open 1NT if my spades were stronger or much weaker.

There is one other point. I expect the field to open 1♠. I don't mind backing my judgment, but since the case is close, I'll try 1♠ like most Souths and hope to pick up matchpoints in the play.

North raises to 2♠, and the opponents pass. My hand has plenty of losers and it wouldn't be the most cowardly pass I ever made, but I hate to mastermind when game is possible. I decide on a general try with 3♣. I could try with 2NT, but I still don't like notrump with this hand.

Partner thinks it over and raises to 4♠. Everyone passes, and West also takes his time before leading the ♠2.

```
              ♠ 9 5 3
              ♥ 6 5 3
              ♦ A 10 4
              ♣ K J 6 4


              ♠ K Q 10 6 4
              ♥ K 4
              ♦ K J 3
              ♣ A 5 2
```

WEST	NORTH	EAST	SOUTH
			1♠
Pass	2♠	Pass	3♣
Pass	4♠	All Pass	

75

North thought he had a maximum, but I don't like his 4♠ much. Since he has bad trumps and no shape, his hand is not as good as its point-count suggests. At least his ♣J is a working card; if he had the ♥J instead, my chances would be gloomier. Maybe I should have passed 2♠.

East takes the ♠A and shifts to the ♥Q. My king loses to West's ace, and a heart comes back to East's ten. I ruff the next heart and draw trumps. East throws a heart; West's trumps were J-7-2.

I'm not a favorite. First I need to win the club finesse, and then I'll need either a 3-3 club break or a guess for the ♦Q. I lead the ♣A and another club, and the queen pops up from West. I take the king and jack, and West discards a heart. When I ruff dummy's last club, West discards a diamond.

Now everyone is down to three diamonds. I know West was 3-4-4-2; that makes him a slim favorite to hold any particular diamond, so I'd finesse through West if I had nothing else to go on. Actually, I have a better reason to place West with the ♦Q. We had a tentative auction to game, suggesting we'd bid it with no extra values. Most Wests would have looked for a passive, safe opening lead. West's trump lead wasn't safe, since East could have held Q-x. If West had a worthless diamond holding such as 9-8-5-2, I'd expect him to lead a diamond.

I try a diamond to dummy's ten, and when it wins, I make the contract. The full deal:

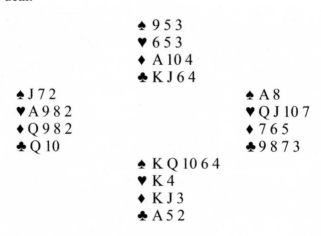

```
                    ♠ 9 5 3
                    ♥ 6 5 3
                    ♦ A 10 4
                    ♣ K J 6 4
    ♠ J 7 2                        ♠ A 8
    ♥ A 9 8 2                      ♥ Q J 10 7
    ♦ Q 9 8 2                      ♦ 7 6 5
    ♣ Q 10                         ♣ 9 8 7 3
                    ♠ K Q 10 6 4
                    ♥ K 4
                    ♦ K J 3
                    ♣ A 5 2
```

We got 10 matchpoints on a 12 top for our +620. If we stay out of game, +170 is worth a 4. Some books say bidding close games at matchpoints doesn't pay. If the play is difficult, the theory goes, you'll get a good score if you make the maximum number of tricks no matter what your contract. In practice, weak defense at many tables will allow shaky games to make. To win a one-session pair event, you must benefit from some of that weak defense.

In a Master Pairs, my partner and I had time for all of five minutes' discussion before gametime. Hence our bidding system, if we can call it that, is skeletal. Our convention card looks as if it took a hit from a bottle of liquid paper.

After three disaster-free rounds, I pick up

♠ A J 2
♥ Q 10 9 6 4 3
♦ 3
♣ A J 8

Both sides are vulnerable, and the dealer, at my right, opens 1NT. His card shows a range of 16 to 18 points.

In a practiced partnership, I might be using a convention with theoretical merit: Cappelletti, Brozel, Astro or whatever. Since my partner and I had no time to go into the ramifications of a complex method, we agreed to play "Mosher." 2♣ shows clubs, 2♦ shows diamonds, double says I can beat it, and so forth. This may not be the soundest way to cope with an opponent's 1NT, but it has the merit of avoiding misunderstandings. I proudly fish the 2♥ card out of my bidding box.

West passes, my partner raises to 3♥ and the opening bidder passes. My hand couldn't be much better. Trade my ♥Q for the ace and I might have risked a penalty double of 1NT, hoping for the magic +200. I have a six-card suit, and I may be able to take winning finesses with my black jacks. I bid 4♥, and everyone passes. Without much thought, West leads the ♦6.

```
          ♠ K 10 7 5 3
          ♥ J 8 5 2
          ♦ Q 5 4
          ♣ 7

          ♠ A J 2
          ♥ Q 10 9 6 4 3
          ♦ 3
          ♣ A J 8
```

WEST	NORTH	EAST	SOUTH
		1NT	2♥
Pass	3♥	Pass	4♥
All Pass			

North's raise to 3♥ was aggressive, but our hands fit well. It looks as if the contract will depend on locating the ♠Q.

I play a low diamond from dummy. East wins with the jack and tries to cash the king, and I ruff. I don't see much chance for a throw-in, but it can't hurt to strip the minor suits. I take the ♣A, ruff a club, ruff dummy's ♦Q (East's ace covers) and ruff my last club. No club honors appear. When I lead a trump next, East takes the king and ace, and West discards a club. East then gets out with another diamond, forcing me to ruff.

Time to guess. East started with the ♥AK and ♦AKJ9. That's 15 points. He needs one black-suit honor to have 16 points but can't have two—that would give him 19 points, too many to open 1NT. Which honor does he have?

I see it. If West had the ♣KQ, his opening lead surely would have been the ♣K instead of a diamond from 10-x-x-x-x. I cash the ♠A and lead the jack, intending to let it ride, and all is well. The full deal:

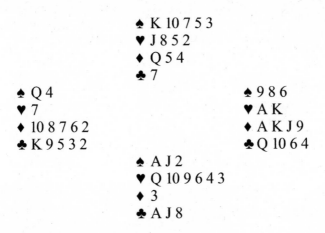

                    ♠ K 10 7 5 3
                    ♥ J 8 5 2
                    ♦ Q 5 4
                    ♣ 7

♠ Q 4   ♠ 9 8 6
♥ 7   ♥ A K
♦ 10 8 7 6 2   ♦ A K J 9
♣ K 9 5 3 2   ♣ Q 10 6 4

                    ♠ A J 2
                    ♥ Q 10 9 6 4 3
                    ♦ 3
                    ♣ A J 8

With four tricks left, the position was

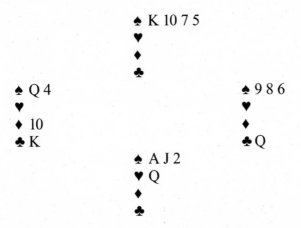

                    ♠ K 10 7 5
                    ♥
                    ♦
                    ♣

♠ Q 4   ♠ 9 8 6
♥   ♥
♦ 10   ♦
♣ K   ♣ Q

                    ♠ A J 2
                    ♥ Q
                    ♦
                    ♣

If I had led my last trump, West would have thrown the ♦10 and East would have had to pitch a spade since to discard the ♣Q would have given away the location of the ♠Q. I expect I'd have guessed right again. East couldn't have started with Q986,AK,AKJ9,1064; West wouldn't have passed over my 2♥ with 4,7,108762,KQ9532.

The defenders couldn't conceal their holdings from declarer in this deal, but as a matter of principle, East should have led the ♦A, not the king, at the second trick. If declarer was about to ruff the second diamond, East had no reason to tell him where the ♦K was.

****

79

As I See It

Oil and Water

Several years ago, my friend Mike Lawrence and I had fun debating the merits of four-card overcalls in Bridge Today magazine. Mike contended, based on his considerable experience, that a four-card overcall was often the best way to initiate a search for a good contract and might offer lead-directing or preemptive benefits as well. I believed, and still do, that a four-card overcall is a misbid that may induce partner to misjudge and may therefore damage partnership trust.

My bias has a basis in fact. In writing for the World Championship books, I saw many results like this one from the 1987 Bermuda Bowl.

```
Dlr: South          ♠ 10 6 5 2
Vul: Both           ♥ A Q 7 6
                    ♦ 4
                    ♣ K 6 4 3
        ♠ Q J 4                      ♠ 8 7
        ♥ K J 9 2                    ♥ 8 4 3
        ♦ A 7 2                      ♦ Q J 10 9 5
        ♣ Q 10 2                     ♣ A 9 7
                    ♠ A K 9 3
                    ♥ 10 5
                    ♦ K 8 6 3
                    ♣ J 8 5
```

WEST	NORTH	EAST	SOUTH
			Pass
1♣	Pass	1♦	1♠
Pass	3♠	All Pass	

North was well worth his raise to 3♠—but only if South had a five-card suit. West found the excellent lead of the ♠J. South and tried a club to dummy's king. East took the ace and returned a trump, and South managed seven tricks for -200.

As seen here, a four-card overcall often lands declarer at a 4-4 or 4-3 fit with minimum high-card values. But if the opening leader has a smattering of high cards (perhaps opposite a partner who has opened the bidding), that is precisely when he'll find a trump lead that may be a killer.

Most good players are willing to overcall occasionally in a four-card suit at the one level. Some of the same players, though, have sworn allegiance to the ubiquitous "Law" of Total Tricks, which states that the total number of trumps both sides have in their best trump suit equals the number of total tricks available. If North-South have nine spades and East-West have nine hearts, 18 tricks should be available at hearts and spades combined. If East-West can make 4♥, North-South will be down two at 4♠. So, at any rate, says the "Law."

I know that a well timed four-card overcall can be a winner, and I admire the scholarly work by Jean-René Vernes and Larry Cohen on behalf of the Total Tricks concept. But oil and water don't mix, and neither do some theories at bridge.

```
Dlr: South        ♠ Q 10 9
Vul: N-S          ♥ K J 3
IMPs              ♦ 3 2
                  ♣ A 9 5 3 2
      ♠ A K 6 3                    ♠ 8 7 5 4
      ♥ A 7 5 2                    ♥ 9
      ♦ Q 10 9 7                   ♦ A 8 6 5
      ♣ 6                         ♣ J 10 7 4
                  ♠ J 2
                  ♥ Q 10 8 6 4
                  ♦ K J 4
                  ♣ K Q 8
```

WEST	NORTH	EAST	SOUTH
			1♥(!)
1♠	2♠	4♠	Pass
Pass	Dbl	All Pass	

When I watched this deal, West hated to pass with his good hand and tried his luck with a four-card overcall. No doubt he hoped East's hand was short in hearts, as seemed possible, hence long in spades. North's 2♠ cue-bid promised heart support with invitational or better values, and East's premature save at 4♠ was an overreaction to the vulnerability. It was far from clear that North-South could make game.

North hammered 4♠ and led a heart. Dummy produced the singleton heart and four trumps West had hoped for, but he was still doomed. He took the ♥A and led a club, and South won with the queen and led a trump. West won and might have taken nine tricks with a cross-ruff (but best defense could always prevail). Instead he made the reasonable play of running the ♦10. South took the jack and led another trump, and West had to lose a trump, a heart and another diamond for down two, +300 to North-South.

East should have bid only 3♠, suggesting a save if West had a suitable hand. Assuming East-West had nine spades, the "Law" might be vindicated even if North-South had only eight hearts: if 3♠ went down one, 3♥ would be cold.

As it was, though, the four-card overcall led East astray. Even 3♠ wasn't sure to make, and 3♥ would almost surely fail (after a spade lead and a club shift, leading to a ruff; or, even if the defense missed its ruff, if South misguessed in diamonds).

Here's another deal I saw recently in an expert IMP game.

```
Dlr: South          ♠ J 7 6
Vul: Both           ♥ K 9 7 5 3
                    ♦ A 10
                    ♣ J 7 2
      ♠ Q 9 4 3 2                    ♠ A K 10 8
      ♥ A 8 4 2                      ♥ Q J
      ♦ 8 4                          ♦ K J 5 3
      ♣ 8 5                          ♣ 9 6 3
                    ♠ 5
                    ♥ 10 6
                    ♦ Q 9 7 6 2
                    ♣ A K Q 10 4
```

WEST	NORTH	EAST	SOUTH
			1♦
Pass	1♥	1♠(!)	2♣
4♠	Dbl	All Pass	

A less sophisticated player might have passed quietly on the East cards, noticing that he had a fistful of losers and values that were better for defense, especially the ♥QJ. But expert East looked at his 14 points, donned his fur cap and trapped his partner with a 1♠ overcall.

After South freely rebid his second suit despite his high-card minimum, West fell into the trap and leaped to game. The 4♠ bid may have been wrong and was certainly wrong if East had only a four-card suit.

Against 4♠ doubled, South cashed two clubs and shifted to the ♥10. East appeared to be annoyed with himself since he didn't give the play his full attention. He put up the ♥A(!), drew trumps and led a diamond from dummy. North grabbed his ace and cashed the ♥K. East then produced his best action of the deal when he claimed nine tricks despite having only eight – and North-South accepted the claim!

What if East passed over 1♥? South would rebid 2♣, and North would take a 2♦ preference. If East passed again, he'd be -90 at worst. If instead he was willing to risk a "pre-balancing" bid of 2♠, he might buy the contract for +110. North-South could take ten tricks at clubs but might not find their eight-card fit.

Pick your theories with care; mix them with greater care. Larry Cohen, who should know better than anyone, has written that he is no fan of four-card overcalls.

Ups and Downs

One of the taxing things about bridge is that success is transitory. In the 15 minutes it takes to play two deals, you can go — forgive me a mixed metaphor — from the penthouse to the outhouse faster than a speeding bullet.

When I watched these two deals. North-South were experts, and North, in fact, had won a world title. On the first deal, North-South had a beautiful result.

```
Dlr: South        ♠ A K 6 4
Vul: Both         ♥ A J 6 5 4
                  ♦ Q J
                  ♣ A 2
       ♠ 10 7 5 3              ♠ J 2
       ♥ K 9 8 3 2            ♥ Q 10 7
       ♦ 6 3                  ♦ 10 9
       ♣ Q 3                  ♣ K J 9 8 7 4
                  ♠ Q 9 8
                  ♥ —
                  ♦ A K 8 7 5 4 2
                  ♣ 10 6 5
```

WEST	NORTH	EAST	SOUTH
			Pass
Pass	1♥	Pass	2♦
Pass	2♠	Pass	3♦
Pass	6♦	Pass	7♦
All Pass			

I liked South's initial pass — many players would have broken discipline and preempted despite the flaws — and I liked his push to 7♦. South had both top trumps, a seventh diamond and a ♠Q that figured to be (and was) useful.

Against the grand slam, West led the ♣Q, and South gave the contract the care it deserved. He took the ♣A, ruffed a heart, drew trumps with the Q-J, ruffed a heart, led to the ♠K, cashed the ♥A and ruffed a heart. A 4-4 heart break (or the fall of the K-Q) would have provided the 13th trick, but when East discarded, South still had chances. He ran his trumps, and West was squeezed in the majors. Nobody else reached 7♦, and many of the pairs in 6♦ took only 12 tricks, so North-South gained heavily against the field.

Alas, a trip down to the outhouse was coming. These were the North-South cards on the next deal:

Dlr: West   ♠ A Q 7 3
Vul: Both   ♥ 8 7 4 3
              ♦ Q 8 7 5
              ♣ 8

              ♠ K 2
              ♥ K J 9 6
              ♦ A K J 3
              ♣ A 6 5

WEST	NORTH	EAST	SOUTH
Pass	Pass	1♣	Dbl
Pass	2♣	Pass	2♦
Pass	Pass	Pass	Oops!

I'd have bid an honest and uncomplicated 1♠ on the North cards in response to South's double, intending to show the hearts next if there were more bidding, but I can understand North's 2♣ cue-bid. South thought he could mark time with 2♦, but the rest was silence.

North rightly pointed out that South had been obliged to show strength at his second turn. A 3♣ cue-bid was correct. North's cue-bid of 2♣ would have promised another bid if he weren't a passed hand, but not in the actual auction. (Is that how you treat this sequence? Do you know how your regular partner treats it?)

2♦ was not the optimum contract — most North-Souths registered +650 at 4♥ — and North-South gave back much of what they had gained on the first deal. How fleeting is fame!

Can Bridge Be Taught?

"Experience is a hard teacher. She gives the test first and the lesson afterwards." – Cy the Cynic

Can bridge be taught? Silly question, perhaps, like "Who built the Eiffel Tower?" Once I wrote an article (for the ACBL's magazine, which refused to print it), suggesting that no student can learn much about the game in, say, 16 hours of classroom time. Hence a teacher's goal must be to inspire students to pursue the game on their own. To accomplish that, he should teach logical thought processes—not just rules—even at the beginning stage.

Few people can knowledgeably and dispassionately tell other people how to play bridge. (Earlier in this book, I suggested that the skill level among all players has declined; it follows that "expert" status isn't what it used to be.) Many teachers ply their trade on the internet; nevertheless, nobody can teach experience. When I watched this deal, in which East was a teacher and West a pupil, I wondered what East would or could say about the result.

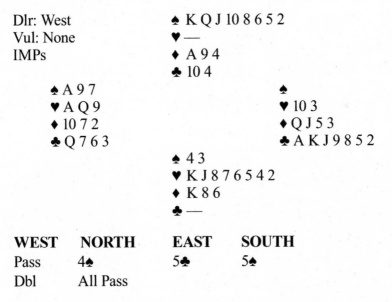

Dlr: West
Vul: None
IMPs

North: ♠ K Q J 10 8 6 5 2　♥ —　♦ A 9 4　♣ 10 4

West: ♠ A 9 7　♥ A Q 9　♦ 10 7 2　♣ Q 7 6 3

East: ♠　♥ 10 3　♦ Q J 5 3　♣ A K J 9 8 5 2

South: ♠ 4 3　♥ K J 8 7 6 5 4 2　♦ K 8 6　♣ —

WEST	NORTH	EAST	SOUTH
Pass	4♠	5♣	5♠
Dbl	All Pass		

When North opened 4♠, teacher East stepped in with 5♣. This is one of those speculative actions we all feel obliged to take. It often turns out badly, but we'll still do it the next time. This time East's action was correct, but only in theory.

South did well to compete with 5♠, and pupil West had to judge. Her good defense, plus a partner who had acted on his own at the five level, suggested doubling for a sure plus; the four cards in clubs suggested bidding.

She doubled and held it to five. East led the ♣K, and North ruffed in dummy and led a low heart: queen, ruff. North ruffed his last club and declined to try for an overtrick by ruffing out West's ♥A. North came to his ♦A to force out the ♠A and lost a diamond at the end.

I don't know what I would have said to West other than "Next time you'll make the winning decision" or "Sorry, I should have passed 4♠."

Can bridge be taught? Experience and judgment can't be taught, but a basis for good judgment can be. This was the next deal:

```
Dlr: North        ♠ 6 3
Vul: N-S          ♥ A Q 10 7
                  ♦ K 10 7 6 5 2
                  ♣ Q
   ♠ Q J 10 9 7 5              ♠ 8 4 2
   ♥ J 9 4 3                   ♥ K 8 5
   ♦ —                         ♦ A Q J 8 4
   ♣ K 10 3                    ♣ 6 2
                  ♠ A K
                  ♥ 6 2
                  ♦ 9 3
                  ♣ A J 9 8 7 5 4
```

WEST	NORTH	EAST	SOUTH
	Pass	Pass	1♣
1♠	Dbl	2♣	3♣
3♠	Pass	4♠	Dbl
All Pass			

My overcalling style wouldn't allow 1♠ on the West cards, but each to his own taste. Most players would have bid 2♦ as North, especially as a passed hand, but perhaps North wanted to get his hearts into the game before East competed in spades.

East's cue-bid promised spade support, and when South bid 3♣, West tried 3♠. Assuming the 1♠ overcall was correct in the partnership style, it's hard to criticize 3♠ since both 3♣ and 3♠ could have been cold. East went

88

on to game, however, and South's double collected 500 points. East then salved his ego by instructing partner that she shouldn't have bid 3♠.

I can indeed see lessons in this deal:

(1) Know your partner's overcalling philosophy.

(2) Don't bid the same values twice. Once East cue-bid, he could have respected West's right to compete for the partscore.

(3) To help your partner judge, bid where you live. East's 2♣ cue-bid with good diamonds and poor spade support was questionable at best. If East bids 2♦ at his second turn, West will be turned off. At worst, East-West will play at 3♠ undoubled for a small loss. More than likely, they will go plus defending against 3NT.

A Hard Slam to Reach

In this internet deal, South and West were professionals, and North and East, I believe, were pupils.

```
Dlr: East          ♠ K J 8 6 5
Vul: N-S           ♥ J 7
IMPs               ♦ 10 8 7 6 2
                   ♣ 4
     ♠ 10 7 4                      ♠ A 2
     ♥ A Q 3                       ♥ K 8 6 5
     ♦ K J 5                       ♦ A 4
     ♣ K J 10 5                    ♣ A Q 7 6 3
                   ♠ Q 9 3
                   ♥ 10 9 4 2
                   ♦ Q 9 3
                   ♣ 9 8 2
```

WEST	NORTH	EAST	SOUTH
		1♣	Pass
2NT	Pass	3♥	Pass
5♣	Pass	6♣	All Pass

Since West's 2NT wasn't Alerted, it must have been natural and forcing. It seems some experts have junked the requirement of stoppers in every unbid suit. After East showed his hearts, West's jump to 5♣ suggested

89

strong clubs and heart help. Some misguided players would think this bid showed no interest in going past game—the dreaded "principle of fast arrival"—but a bid that offers to take 11 tricks can hardly be characterized as discouraging. East really should have tried for seven.

Against 6♣, South led a heart, and East drew trumps and had a free shot by finessing with the ♦J. He claimed 13 tricks.

A 50-50 chance isn't nearly enough to risk a grand slam, so 6♣ was a good contract. To get there seemed routine, and I expected a small swing to East-West. Well, they got a swing, but it wasn't small. When I called up the results, I was amazed.

Dozens of pairs had bid 1NT, 3NT. Even when East happened to notice that he had unbalanced distribution and prime values and opened 1♣, East-West often ran aground, partly because they had no forcing club raise. West usually temporized with 1♦, leading to an auction such as

WEST	NORTH	EAST	SOUTH
		1♣	Pass
1♦	Pass	1♥	Pass
1♠	Pass	2NT	Pass
3NT	All Pass		

Nor did an inverted minor-suit raise necessarily solve the problem. One pair got to slam via 1♣, 2♣-2♥, 4♣-4NT, 5♦-6♣; but at two tables, after 1♣, 2♣, East woodenly jumped to 3NT, passed out.

At other tables, West players leaped to 3NT over 1♣. They weren't bothered by their spades either. Most Easts apparently thought West had about 13 points and passed – a timid view. A few Easts played West for extras and leaped boldly to 6NT, a deecent matchpoint spot. One East jumped to 6♣ over 3NT. Only a couple of Easts investigated with 4NT, 4♣ or 4♥.

I see these pointers:

– Never fear to jump to emphasize an important feature such as good trumps. Edgar Kaplan said it best: "In a slam auction, one jump is worth several delicate minimum forcing bids."

– Hands with prime values are worth more than their point-count. The East hand, with excellent controls, didn't need much help to make slam if West had a club fit.

– Finding a fit is the essence of bidding. To play a system with no forcing minor-suit raise is folly.

– Don't make final decisions too soon. If you think slam is possible, make a try. Find out what your partner thinks.

****

At My Club

Dlr: South	♠ 9 4		
Vul: N-S	♥ A 8 5 2		
	♦ 8 6		
	♣ Q 9 8 7 3		

♠ 10 2	♠ Q J 8 7
♥ K J 9 6 4 3	♥ Q 10 7
♦ K 4 3 2	♦ J 9
♣ 10	♣ K 6 5 4

♠ A K 6 5 3
♥ —
♦ A Q 10 7 5
♣ A J 2

WEST	NORTH	EAST	SOUTH
			1♠
Pass	1NT	Pass	3♦
Pass	3♠	Pass	4♦
Pass	4♠	All Pass	

"I've begged and pleaded and offered my services free, but she's as obstinate as death."

Dr. Ed Fitch, our club president, was talking about Minnie Bottoms; her old bifocals make her mix up kings and jacks, often to her opponents' chagrin. Ed, an ophthalmologist, has tried to get Minnie to accept a new prescription for glasses.

"She thinks her old ones are lucky," Ed sighed.

"She may be right," I said.

Minnie's glasses had won a match in a team event. At both tables South landed at 4♠, and West led the ♣10. Dummy's queen won, and South threw his ♣J on the ♥A and led a diamond: nine, queen ...

At one table West took the king and led a heart, and South ruffed and cashed the ♦A. When the jack fell, South took the A-K of trumps and led good diamonds. He lost two trumps and a diamond.

"Minnie was West at the other table," Ed told me, "and when South finessed with the ♦Q, Minnie played low!"

"She thought her king was the jack," I smiled.

"South cashed the ♦A," Ed went on, "and when the jack fell, he could've taken the A-K of trumps and forced out the ♦K. But South hated to pass up a 'sure' overtrick. He ruffed a diamond, expecting 'East's' king to fall."

South was stunned when East overruffed and gave Minnie a club ruff. Minnie then led a trump, and South had to lose a diamond to her king and a trump to East. Down one.

****

Sit Beside Me

My judgment is rusty, and my competitive decisions sometimes display the delicate touch of a gorilla, but this deal pleased me. In a Regional IMP Pairs, I'm East with a promising hand:

♠ A K Q 10 4
♥ A Q 2
♦ K 3
♣ K 7 2

Both sides are vulnerable. My partner deals and passes, and I start to wonder whether I should open 2NT or try 1♠. These days, some players are opening 2NT with shaded values — sometimes with 19 good points — and they might like this hand enough to start with 2♣. But Edgar Kaplan warned against being eager to start with 2NT. He argued that 2NT is a space-consuming action; a suit opening bid will allow an easier auction if partner doesn't pass – and there won't be many hands with which he will respond to 2NT yet pass one of a suit.

What I'd have done I'll never know. North, in second seat, opens 1♠ in front of me!

I must act. To hope it will go Pass-Pass-Dbl by West is rather too much to hope for, and we may have a game. So I double, intending to bid notrump next. South bids 2♥, my partner passes and North rebids 2NT.

I doubt they can make that, but I can't be sure of beating it badly. I won't be able to run the spades, and South has a heart suit sitting behind my A-Q-2. Moreover, West is marked with nothing. North opened—give him 12 points — and South bid — give him seven. How many are left for West?

I pass, and South tries 3♣. North considers and passes. For all I know, they're cold for 4♣, and I can see no spot for us; so despite my 21-count, I pass. West leads the ♠2, and a featherweight dummy hits.

```
              ♠ J 8 7 6 3
              ♥ 8
              ♦ A Q 9 7
              ♣ A 8 4

                   N              ♠ A K Q 10 4
              W  ─┼─  E           ♥ A Q 2
                   S              ♦ K 3
                                  ♣ K 7 2
```

WEST	NORTH	EAST	SOUTH
Pass	1♠	Dbl	2♥
Pass	2NT	Pass	3♣
All Pass			

I take the ♠10, cash the ♠A and shift, perhaps questionably, to a low trump: three, jack from West, ace. When dummy leads a heart next, I grab the ace and lead the ♣K and another club. Declarer loses another heart, going down one.

```
              ♠ J 8 7 6 3
              ♥ 8
              ♦ A Q 9 7
              ♣ A 8 4
  ♠ 2                          ♠ A K Q 10 4
  ♥ 10 7 6 3                   ♥ A Q 2
  ♦ 10 8 6 5 4 2               ♦ K 3
  ♣ J 5                        ♣ K 7 2
              ♠ 9 5
              ♥ K J 9 5 4
              ♦ J
              ♣ Q 10 9 6 3
```

We might do better if I continue spades at the third trick (although declarer could ruff with the ♣Q effectively). Perhaps I should have played West for an honor in trumps since otherwise he might have led a trump as the bidding suggested, but I felt that a trump shift was likely to beat 3♣.

I settled for +100 on my mammoth hand, but we still gained IMPs. At many tables, my hand couldn't resist bidding notrump with all those points. West ran to diamonds, whereupon East usually bid even more notrump and went minus.

Players are often afraid to retire from the auction with a strong hand, but here my passes were clear. I had no reason to believe that the opponents were fooling around or that my side could make anything.

Never be afraid to back your judgment in the auction. You may be going against the field, but so what? The field never won an event.

In a Regional pair event, my partner never met a hand he didn't like, but my style is more conservative. Our opponents are competent. On the first board of the round, they reached a good game and made it. Then as South I pick up

♠ Q J 10
♥ A 9 8 6 3
♦ 6
♣ A 8 6 3

Both sides are vulnerable, and East opens 1♦. I'd rather have more values, but I can't stay out of this auction with a near-opening bid and shortness in diamonds. Some players would double, but I prefer a 1♥ overcall. My hand isn't strong enough to double and then bid hearts, and unless I get my five-card suit mentioned, we may lose a 5-3 heart fit. If my partner has spades, maybe he'll bid them.

Instead, West responds 1♠, and North raises me to 2♥. East doubles. That's a "support" double: East has three cards in spades. I pass, West corrects to 2♠ and North competes with 3♥. Everyone passes, and West leads the ♦J.

♠ A 3
♥ 10 7 4
♦ 9 7 4 3
♣ K J 10 2

♠ Q J 10
♥ A 9 8 6 3
♦ 6
♣ A 8 6 3

WEST	NORTH	EAST	SOUTH
		1♦	1♥
1♠	2♥	Dbl	Pass
2♠	3♥	All Pass	

North's 3♥ with three low trumps was bold, but he knows I prefer to overcall sound, and he liked his hand (as usual). He has no wasted honors in diamonds and doubtless thinks I have length in clubs so his clubs honors will be useful. His judgment was on target this time, so I need to make him look good.

East takes the ♦A and returns a low diamond, and I ruff. Nobody doubled 3♥ so I expect the trumps will break, but I'm still off a diamond, two trumps and probably a spade. This deal will come down to a guess for the ♣Q.

To start, I'll find out about the spades. I let the ♠Q ride, and East takes the king and leads another diamond. I ruff again and lead a low trump, saving the ace to keep control. East wins with the jack and leads a fourth diamond. I ruff with my last low trump, and West follows with the king.

When I cash the ♥A, West plays the queen and East plays low. East, I imagine, has the king left, but since all the diamonds have been played, I can find out safely. I cross to the ♠A and lead dummy's last trump. East wins, and West throws a spade. East then returns a spade to my jack.

I've put it off as long as possible. Three tricks are left: I have ♣KJ10 in dummy and ♣A86 in my hand. Which way to finesse?

I almost know East's exact hand. He had ♠Kxx, ♥KJx, ♦AQxx, and three clubs. I check their convention card for their 1NT range. It's 15 to

17, so my problem is solved. If East had the ♣Q, he'd have a balanced 15 points.

I take the ♣A and lead a club, intending to finesse with the jack, and all is well. The full deal is:

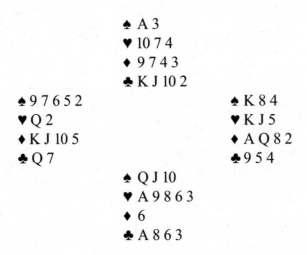

```
                  ♠ A 3
                  ♥ 10 7 4
                  ♦ 9 7 4 3
                  ♣ K J 10 2
  ♠ 9 7 6 5 2                    ♠ K 8 4
  ♥ Q 2                          ♥ K J 5
  ♦ K J 10 5                     ♦ A Q 8 2
  ♣ Q 7                          ♣ 9 5 4
                  ♠ Q J 10
                  ♥ A 9 8 6 3
                  ♦ 6
                  ♣ A 8 6 3
```

Our matchpoint result for +140 was good. Some North-Souths sold out to 2♠ for -110. When North-South bid 3♥, not many East-Wests competed to 3♠, and those who did played undoubled for -100.

All I had to do in the play was delay the crucial club guess until the end. My plays in spades and trumps acted as "discovery" plays. I was actively looking for information to let me place the ♣Q.

I am perplexed when I see a reputable bridge teacher assail new players with "eight ever, nine never." My feeling is that unless beginners see quickly that bridge offers more than the application of rules, they'll look elsewhere for a source of intellectual pleasure. But if teachers are going to disgorge rules, at least they ought to pick one with more basis in fact. With nine cards in a suit missing the queen, the odds that favor playing for the drop are tiny. With any indication from the bidding or play, finesse instead; if there is no indication, look for one.

As South in a Sectional Open Pairs, I pick up

♠ A K J
♥ 8 4 2
♦ A K Q 3
♣ A 8 4

East passes. This is my idea of a 2NT opening: 21 good high-card points. I often see players fudge on 2NT openings—19 reasonable points seem to be tempting—but I never go out of my way to open 2NT and start the search for our best contract at the three level. If my ♣A were the king, I'd open 1♦.

With my actual hand, the lack of a heart stopper is no deterrent; I just need balanced distribution. So I open 2NT, and my partner raises to 3NT. Everyone passes, and West leads the ♠2 (fourth best).

♠ 8 4
♥ Q 10
♦ 9 7 6
♣ K J 10 9 6 3

♠ A K J
♥ 8 4 2
♦ A K Q 3
♣ A 8 4

WEST	NORTH	EAST	SOUTH
		Pass	2NT
Pass	3NT	All Pass	

At IMPs, I might prefer to be at 5♣. If the opening lead were, say, a diamond, declarer could win and cash the ♣AK. If the queen didn't fall, he might try the diamonds, succeeding with a 3-3 break. If diamonds broke 4-2 but nobody ruffed the third diamond, declarer could ruff the fourth diamond and try the spade finesse as a last resort.

Since it's matchpoints, my partner gave no thought to the minor-suit game. We can't afford to play at 5♣ when 3NT may produce +720.

East puts up the ♠Q, and I win and cash the ♣A. Both defenders play low. I can lead a second club to the king, relying on "nine never," but first I try the top diamonds. If the diamonds break 3-3, I have nine tricks. I may still need the clubs for a good matchpoint score, but at the least, I'll get some information.

West follows twice in diamonds, then discards a low heart.

I know West had four spades—he led the deuce—and two diamonds. He can't have as many as five hearts. Then he'd have led a heart against 3NT. So West must have three clubs.

When I lead another club, West plays low, and I finesse with the jack and wind up taking 12 tricks. The full deal:

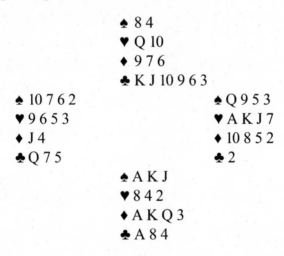

```
                    ♠ 8 4
                    ♥ Q 10
                    ♦ 9 7 6
                    ♣ K J 10 9 6 3
   ♠ 10 7 6 2                      ♠ Q 9 5 3
   ♥ 9 6 5 3                       ♥ A K J 7
   ♦ J 4                           ♦ 10 8 5 2
   ♣ Q 7 5                         ♣ 2
                    ♠ A K J
                    ♥ 8 4 2
                    ♦ A K Q 3
                    ♣ A 8 4
```

Some partners are hard to please. I was happy with my play, but my partner wasn't – and wasn't too observant. When I finessed on the second club, he apparently assumed I had A-x ("eight ever"), and when I followed suit to the third club, he didn't notice.

"Take your spades and run the clubs before you cash the diamonds," he chastised me, "and you squeeze East in the red suits and take 13 tricks."

I'm playing with an old friend in a casual internet game. My partner is a good player, and our opponents have described themselves as "advanced." What this often means, I've found, is that they know lots of conventions.

With only our side vulnerable, I'm South with

♠ 8 6 4 2
♥ A Q 7 5 3 2
♦ Q 6
♣ 7

My partner opens 1NT, and East doubles, conventionally showing a one-suited hand. West is supposed to bid 2♣, after which East will usually bid his suit or pass if he has clubs.

My partner and I agreed to play transfers but didn't discuss whether to use them over interference. I don't know whether I can transfer to hearts or bid 2♣, Stayman. To avoid a disastrous misunderstanding, I start with a "safety call": redouble. There are two passes, and East runs to 2♣.

I could bid 4♥ now, but I'm still afraid partner might think I have spades. Besides, 4♥ may not be best. North could have only two hearts and four or even five spades. So I cue-bid 3♣. Partner bids 3♦, denying a four-card major, and now I think I can try 4♥.

Everyone passes, and West leads the ♣9.

♠ K J 9
♥ 10 4
♦ A K 10 5 3
♣ A J 5

♠ 8 6 4 2
♥ A Q 7 5 3 2
♦ Q 6
♣ 7

WEST	NORTH	EAST	SOUTH
	1NT	Dbl	Redbl
Pass	Pass	2♣	3♣
Pass	3♦	Pass	4♥
All Pass			

Not bad. I have a chance unless the trumps go sour. I take the ♣A, and East follows with the deuce. A low trump from dummy goes to East's six,

102

my queen and West's king. West leads another club, and I ruff East's ten and cash the ♥A. West plays the eight and East the jack.

I have a straightforward line from here. I can take the top diamonds. If the jack falls, I continue diamonds, pitching two spades. The worst that can happen is that West ruffs and leads a spade, forcing me into a guess for the contract. If instead West turns up with four diamonds to the jack, I can ruff a fourth diamond, lead a spade myself and hope to guess right.

The more I think about it, though, I'm convinced that play will fail. West surely has the missing high trump, and East's ♣2 at the first trick troubles me. East was begging for a shift—obviously to spades—and wouldn't be eager for a spade shift if he had only the ace. I think my only chance is to pitch three spades before West can ruff. That means West must hold four diamonds, and then the odds are he'll have the jack.

I take the ♦Q and lead another diamond. West plays the deuce and then the nine, but I finesse with the ten. East follows low—and shows out on the ♦K! Goodness, I'm going to make it. I pitch spades on the ♦K, ♦A and fifth diamond. West ruffs, but the defense gets only one spade and two trumps. The full deal:

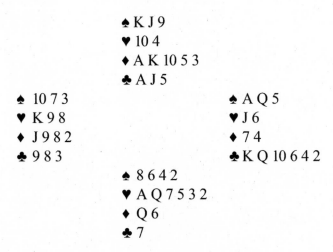

```
              ♠ K J 9
              ♥ 10 4
              ♦ A K 10 5 3
              ♣ A J 5
  ♠ 10 7 3                    ♠ A Q 5
  ♥ K 9 8                     ♥ J 6
  ♦ J 9 8 2                   ♦ 7 4
  ♣ 9 8 3                     ♣ K Q 10 6 4 2
              ♠ 8 6 4 2
              ♥ A Q 7 5 3 2
              ♦ Q 6
              ♣ 7
```

"You sure are lucky," my partner types. He's right.

Deals on which declarer must make an assumption about the way the missing cards lie are common. To finesse with the ♦10 was scary, but I was following the consequences of my assumptions.

As for the defense, West should have trusted East's signal. Since East had many clubs from which to choose, the deuce sent a clear message: "If you get in, shift!"

****

As I See It

Loose Lips

The mean age of ACBL members, if not that of those who play on the internet, has risen. Some players will remember the injunction that appeared on posters in defense plants during World War II: "Loose Lips Sink Ships" referred to maintaining tight security. I can't say I recall it — even in 1945 I was only a gleam in my father's eye — but I know unzipped lips can sink the defense at the bridge table.

```
Dlr: South          ♠ 7 6
Vul: E-W            ♥ 9 6 4
IMPs               ♦ J 10 7 2
                   ♣ J 10 6 5
      ♠ A 2                      ♠ Q J 9 5
      ♥ K 10 5                   ♥ A J 8 3 2
      ♦ Q 9 6                    ♦ A
      ♣ Q 9 7 4 3                ♣ A K 2
                   ♠ K 10 8 4 3
                   ♥ Q 7
                   ♦ K 8 5 4 3
                   ♣ 8
```

WEST	NORTH	EAST	SOUTH
			Pass
Pass	Pass	1♥	2♥
4♥	Pass	4NT	Pass
5♥	5NT	6♥	All Pass

When I watched this deal, South was one of the nation's top junior players. North wasn't as strong and, as you'll see, neither were East and West.

South's 2♥ was a Michaels cue-bid, promising length in spades and a minor suit. I didn't care much for that call: North-South were unlikely to buy the contract, especially when North had passed, and South's bid would give East-West a blueprint of the distribution. South's bid did have one possible upside: if East-West landed at a heart contract, East would be apt to mis-guess the queen of trumps.

West should have started with a double to show strength before supporting the hearts. His jump to 4♥ suggested more hearts, better distribution and fewer high-card values. Nevertheless, East diagnosed his partner's hand and continued with 4NT, Key Card Blackwood.

When West responded 5♥, showing two Key Cards, North thought it was time to suggest a save with 5NT. Since there was no certainty 6♥ would make even if it was bid, this action was rash, and East could have accepted the fielder's choice by doubling. He'd have collected +1400 against 6♦ doubled, but instead he plunged on with 6♥.

South led the ♣8; no lead was attractive. East took the ace and promptly led a trump to dummy's ten! He picked up the trumps, set up the clubs and lost one spade at the end.

Some of the other kibitzers, who had expected declarer to go down, were amazed and said so, but North's bid of 5NT had tipped off the trump position. If North had the queen, he wouldn't have been tempted to save.

When I see a result such as this—East-West had only 30 high-card points and were off a key queen, a key king and some handling—I always wonder what would have happened if North-South kept their lips tightly zipped. It's easy to construct an unobstructed East-West auction to reach 6♥, and just as easy to construct one that reasonably stops at game.

As often happens, the North-South "interference" spurred East-West to bid with all the more determination to slam—and then helped them make it.

Preferential Treatment

I'm a big believer in showing support for partner's suit. Suppose you hold

♠ J 7 6 ♥ A J 7 ♦ K Q 9 6 ♣ A J 5.

You open 1NT, and your partner responds 3♠, natural and forcing. Some players would persist with 3NT because of the balanced distribution and mediocre spades. A disciplined player raises to 4♠, which is what his partner wants him to do with three-card or better support.

In a Bermuda Bowl many years ago, a U.S. pair held these cards:

WEST	EAST
♠ A 4	♠ Q J 7 2
♥ A 6 4	♥ 10
♦ A Q 9 7 3	♦ K J 6
♣ 10 8 2	♣ A K Q 7 6
1♦	2♣
2NT	3♠
3NT	Pass

The auction was a sad display. West refused to bid 4♣ over 3♠ even though he had a fine hand for play at clubs. East never showed his diamond support; perhaps 3♦ over 2NT wouldn't have been forcing, but then East could have tried 4♦ over 3NT.

In spite of all that, showing support or taking a preference can be a doubtful action. Compare these two auctions

WEST	EAST
1♦	1♠
2♣	2♥

WEST	EAST
1♦	1♠
2♣	3♦ (invitational)

107

In the first auction, East has bid two suits and invites West to take a spade preference. If West holds

♠ Q 6   ♥ 7 6   ♦ A Q 8 5 3   ♣ A K 6 5,

he can bid 2♠. But in the second auction, East has supported West's first suit and is less interested in hearing a preference. Therefore, a 3♠ bid should show better support. West should bid 4♦ or 5♦.

As West you hold

♠ A 9 6 3   ♥ J 7 4   ♦ K Q 9 4   ♣ K 6.

WEST	EAST
1♦	1♥
1♠	1NT

Pass, don't bid 2♥. You can't bid three times with this minimum hand. If your hand were

♠ A 9 6 3   ♥ K Q 3   ♦ K 9 6 4   ♣ 7 6,

you could make a case for raising East's 1♥ response to 2♥.

In the deal below, from an internet game, North made a questionable decision.

```
Dlr: South         ♠ A 8 5
Vul: E-W           ♥ Q 10 2
                   ♦ K 9 8 2
                   ♣ K Q 3
    ♠ J 9 2                          ♠ 10 7 4
    ♥ A 8 5 4 3                      ♥ K J 6
    ♦ A 4                            ♦ 6 5 3
    ♣ 10 9 4                         ♣ A J 7 6
                   ♠ K Q 6 3
                   ♥ 9 7
                   ♦ Q J 10 7
                   ♣ 8 5 2
```

WEST	NORTH	EAST	SOUTH
			Pass
Pass	1♦	Pass	1♠
Pass	1NT	Pass	2♦
Pass	2♠	All Pass	

North had an excuse for his 2♠ bid: the game was matchpoints. Even so, he hadn't been asked to take a preference, 2♦ rated to be a safer contract, and a plus score in a delicate partscore deal can be worth a lot.

Against 2♠, West led the ♥A, a happy choice for him, and continued hearts. South ruffed the third heart and led the ♦Q, and West took the ace and led a fourth heart. Declarer ruffed in dummy with the eight, East uppercut with the ten, and South put herself in a hopeless position when she overruffed with the queen.

South next led a club to the queen, and East ducked. After a diamond back to the jack, South led a trump to the ace and perversely tried another diamond. West ruffed and persisted with his last heart, ruffed in dummy with the five. East overruffed again, with the seven, and South consigned herself to down two by overruffing with the king. +100 to East-West.

South could make 2♠ by pitching on the fourth heart instead of overruffing East. But West could always beat the contract by ducking the first diamond, threatening declarer with a diamond ruff. It seems North might have done well to pass 2♦, accepting a mundane +90.

Gain vs. Loss

You're South in a Team Trials, both sides vulnerable, and pick up

♠ K 8 3
♥ A J 9 6 5
♦ Q 6
♣ A 9 8

North deals and passes, and East opens 1♠. Would you bid? Suppose you knew your worst nightmare was a reality: West has a heart stack you wouldn't believe. Would you act then?

I was watching a strong IMP game when a South player faced a similar problem—if indeed you'd deem it a problem. With both sides vulnerable, East, the dealer, opened 1♠. South held

♠ A 9 8 3
♥ K J 8 7 6
♦ A 8
♣ J 4

I thought South should bid. True, the result could be catastrophic, but if North has a heart fit, North-South may have a game. (An optimist — somebody who expects a new box of corn flakes to be half full, not half empty — places North with spade shortness and therefore heart support. South can't count on that, of course, but there is no law against hoping.) Moreover, a 2♥ overcall has obstructive value.

If South held

♠ A 9 8 3
♥ J 4
♦ A 8
♣ K J 8 7 6,

2♣ would have less to gain. Even if North has club support, game at clubs is far away – and if it's a partscore deal and North has clubs, East-West may have a red-suit fit and will have an edge in the auction.

What happened? South passed. West responded 1NT, and East rebid 2♠. South passed again, and so did everyone else.

```
                    ♠ 10
                    ♥ Q 10 9 5
                    ♦ 9 6 4 2
                    ♣ A 10 7 5
      ♠ Q 7                        ♠ K J 6 5 4 2
      ♥ 4 2                        ♥ A 3
      ♦ Q 10 7                     ♦ K J 5 3
      ♣ K Q 8 6 3 2                ♣ 9
                    ♠ A 9 8 3
                    ♥ K J 8 7 6
                    ♦ A 8
                    ♣ J 4
```

110

South led the ♣J, and North took dummy's king and shifted to the ♠10, passed to dummy's queen. Declarer then threw his losing heart on the ♣Q and continued trumps for +140. After South led a club, no defense would beat 3♠, and North-South were assured of a loss: they could make 4♥.

It was right to bid on the first hand as well—even with North a passed hand. Edgar Kaplan overcalled 2♥. Later, he wrote that he detested overcalling on a ragged suit but considered it more dangerous to pass. He weighed the risk—the poor suit quality—against the plentiful high cards and controls and judged that the chance of game justified action. The full deal:

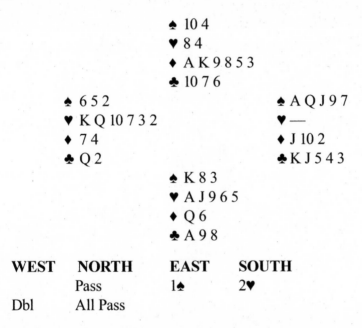

```
                    ♠ 10 4
                    ♥ 8 4
                    ♦ A K 9 8 5 3
                    ♣ 10 7 6
      ♠ 6 5 2                      ♠ A Q J 9 7
      ♥ K Q 10 7 3 2               ♥ —
      ♦ 7 4                        ♦ J 10 2
      ♣ Q 2                        ♣ K J 5 4 3
                    ♠ K 8 3
                    ♥ A J 9 6 5
                    ♦ Q 6
                    ♣ A 9 8
```

WEST	NORTH	EAST	SOUTH
	Pass	1♠	2♥
Dbl	All Pass		

West led a spade, and East took the ace and shifted to a club. Kaplan won the second club, cashed the ♠K, ruffed a spade and took three high diamonds, pitching his last club. West, down to his six trumps, ruffed and led the ♥K. Kaplan played low, won the next trump cheaply and exited with a trump, forcing West to pitch back into the ♥AJ and concede the doubled contract. (Only the lead of the ♣Q would beat 2♥.)

In judging whether to make a doubtful overcall at IMPs, weigh your chances for game.

****

At My Club

One stormy November afternoon — it was still two years before Bill Frump would get his final comeuppance — I had a game with Ed Fitch, the ophthalmologist who presides over our club. The deals were dull that day, and little of interest happened for seven rounds. Then Frump arrived with his partner, a visiting expert, in tow.

When someone passing through the city called up Mabel, our manager, in search of a game, she often enlisted Bill. Though he had no doubt that our members had the collective card sense of a plank and was intolerable when partnering one of them, Bill put stock in the old definition of an expert — someone from out of town — and could be relied on to act halfway civil to a visitor.

Bill didn't introduce his partner. He took his cards out of the tray, looked at them as if he was a teacher and they were a class of unruly students, and fished the one-spade card out of his bidding box. The V.E. responded 1NT and played there. It was hard work, but declarer got home with an endplay.

"Your partner knows the game," I remarked to Bill. He grunted something unintelligible and reached for his next hand.

Dlr: West   ♠ 8 2
Vul: None   ♥ Q 8 3
                 ♦ K 9 3
                 ♣ A 10 6 4 2

♠ 5 3   ♠ K Q J 10 6
♥ J 6 5 4 2   ♥ K 10 9
♦ 7 6 5   ♦ 10 4 2
♣ K 9 7   ♣ Q 8

                 ♠ A 9 7 4
                 ♥ A 7
                 ♦ A Q J 8
                 ♣ J 5 3

WEST	NORTH	EAST	SOUTH
F.S.	Frump	Dr. Ed	V.E.
Pass	Pass	1♠	1NT
Pass	3NT	All Pass	

I led a spade, and the V.E. won the second round. After a modest pause, he went for a swindle, leading a diamond to dummy and returning the ♣2. Ed played low, for which I couldn't blame him, and declarer played the jack.

I ducked to shut out the clubs (I'm still not sure what my optimum strategy is, but I'll bet that if I'd taken the king, this declarer would have played Ed for Q-8 because of his opening bid and made an overtrick.) The V.E. then took the ♣A and the rest of the diamonds and exited with a spade. In the end, Ed had to lead from the ♥K, and the contract was made.

Nobody said a word. As Bill reached for his private score, I wondered if he'd ever complimented a partner's play in his life. (I fear I'd have tried a club to the ace at the third trick, hoping for a singleton honor offside. Then a diamond back and a low club would oblige West to duck, setting up the same ending.)

Frump wrote down 400 in the plus column and 90 just above that and idly scanned his card as players will do. And then I saw his eyes widen, and the intake of his breath came as sharp as a razor's edge.

The plus side of his score was full of numbers; the minus column was empty.

Four months earlier, attendance at the club had been suffering, perhaps because Frump had been playing more than usual. Dr. Ed had what seemed a perfect solution.

"We offer a $20,000 prize to any member who has a session with all plus scores," he told our Board. "We call it 'The Perfect Game'. We always have at least nine tables with 27 boards in play, so it'll be just like a perfect game in baseball: 27 up and 27 down."

"What if somebody wins?" Henrietta frowned. "We don't have that kind of money."

Ed had an answer to that. "We've got, what, a hundred members? We'd assess them $200 apiece. Everybody will have a chance to win. And what are the odds against all plus scores anyway? A billion to one?"

"I've never heard of it happening," I said.

"Oh dear," sighed Henrietta; but she voted yes, along with everyone else. The Perfect Game was posted, attendance zoomed and Ed was hailed as a genius.

The third board was predictable. The V.E. opened 1♠, and Frump passed with 14 points and four trumps. We got a top I'd have traded for a bottom, and Frump needed three more plus scores to pitch his perfect game.

The last round was a bye round for us. "If you know any prayers," I told Ed, "dust them off. Frump has 24 plus scores."

He looked at me as if I'd passed him a live hand grenade. "The members will kill me," he groaned. "If it were anybody but that Frump, they might let me off with a caning. Whom does he play on the last round?"

"Henrietta," I said. "And Minnie."

Minnie Bottoms was 81. In those days she never missed a session despite her poor eyesight—and she already wielded the ancient bifocals that made her confuse kings and jacks, often to her opponents' chagrin.

Ed and I pulled up chairs. I didn't dare say anything. Minnie, who'd had open-heart surgery twice, didn't know what pressure at the bridge table was, but Henrietta was always nervous when she played against Frump.

Dlr: West
Vul: None

```
                    ♠ A Q 8 6 5
                    ♥ Q 3
                    ♦ 7 5 4
                    ♣ A 5 2
    ♠ K J                              ♠ 10 9 7 4
    ♥ 8                                ♥ J 10 5 4
    ♦ K Q J 9 3                        ♦ 10 8 2
    ♣ K Q 10 9 4                       ♣ J 6
                    ♠ 3 2
                    ♥ A K 9 7 6 2
                    ♦ A 6
                    ♣ 8 7 3
```

Minnie's table didn't use bidding boxes, so we heard this auction:

WEST	NORTH	EAST	SOUTH
Minnie	V.E.	Henrietta	Frump
1♦	1♠	Pass	2♥
3♣	Pass	3♦	3♥
4♣(!)	4♥	All Pass	

Minnie led the ♦J (thinking it was the king). Frump didn't like his dummy, but he took the ace and led a spade, resigned to the finesse since he needed it to have a chance. Minnie played the king.

"Beautiful," I whispered to Ed. "He's sure Minnie has ten minor-suit cards, and now he has a chance to mis-guess in trumps."

Frump won the ♠A. With the anxiety building on his face, he led the queen and another trump. And Henrietta split her honors!

116

Ed buried his face in his hands.

Frump cackled when Minnie showed out. In short order, he took the
♠Q, ruffed a spade, went to the ♣A, ruffed a spade, exited with a club and
claimed two more tricks with the A-9 of trumps. We had two chances
left.

```
Dlr: South          ♠ 7 3
Vul: None           ♥ A Q 9
                    ♦ 10 9 6 5 3 2
                    ♣ 6 3
      ♠ A J 9 8 5 2              ♠ Q 10
      ♥ K 6 4                    ♥ 8 7 5 2
      ♦ K J                      ♦ 8 7
      ♣ 8 4                      ♣ J 10 9 7 5
                    ♠ K 6 4
                    ♥ J 10 3
                    ♦ A Q 4
                    ♣ A K Q 2
```

WEST	NORTH	EAST	SOUTH
Minnie	V.E.	Henrietta	Frump
			1NT(!)
2♠	2NT	Pass	Pass
Pass			

Frump's 1NT was a deliberate underbid, of course. The V.E.'s 2NT
was Lebensohl; he wanted to sign off at 3♦. But Frump had too many
dollar signs dancing in his head to remember his methods.

Minnie led a spade, and Frump took the king.

"We have a shot," I muttered to Ed. "If he tries to combine his chances,
we have a shot."

After what seemed an eternity, Frump laid down the ♦A. Minnie
played the king.

"We may have him," Ed said. "He may go over with the ♥A to lead
the ♦10."

Frump pulled out the ♦Q and slapped it defiantly on the table.

"Good thing I was declarer," Bill told the V.E. smugly as he entered +270. "You don't know Minnie like I do."

Minnie gave him an indignant look. But Bill needed one plus for the $20,000. I glanced at Ed; he resembled an overused washrag.

The first two deals had taken an age, and the other tables had finished. Word of Frump's attempt to match Don Larsen had spread, and players hovered around the table like investors watching the bottom fall out of a once-promising market.

Henrietta looked bewildered. With the chips on the table, fate dealt Minnie a balanced 25-count. (Directions changed)

```
Dlr: South          ♠ 8 3
Vul: N-S            ♥ 5 4 2
                    ♦ 6 4 2
                    ♣ K 10 6 4 2
       ♠ K J 4                      ♠ 10 9 7 5 2
       ♥ Q 10 8 6                   ♥ 9
       ♦ K Q J 7 3                  ♦ 10 9 5
       ♣ 5                          ♣ 9 8 7 3
                    ♠ A Q 6
                    ♥ A K J 7 3
                    ♦ A 8
                    ♣ A Q J
```

Minnie opened 2♣ on the South cards, and the V.E. bid 2♦. Pass, Pass, ...

Bid notrump, Minnie, I telegraphed silently. It was too much to hope she would pass.

"Two hearts."

Strike one.

West passed, and Henrietta, her face as taut as piano wire, raised to 3♥.

Strike two.

Oh Lord, Minnie, I begged, please bid 3NT.

"Three notrump."

Ed exhaled and sat back in his chair. But after the V.E. passed, Henrietta started to think.

"I don't believe this," I whispered to Ed as the seconds ticked by.

"Four hearts."

There was a clearly audible moan from the kibitzers. "We're toast," Ed said matter-of-factly.

When he and I had played the deal, we had reached 4♥, and I'd won the second diamond and cashed the A-K of trumps. When East showed out, I led another trump, but West won and forced with a diamond. Since I couldn't lead a fourth trump, I started the clubs. West ruffed the third club and led another diamond, and I lost two spades. No other play, I consoled myself, would have prevailed against the best defense.

We watched as the V.E. led the ♦K. Minnie played low, won the next diamond – and led the jack of trumps. The V.E. took his queen and led a high diamond.

"Lead out of turn," murmured Minnie. "The last trick was mine."

"You led the jack, he took the queen," Frump said impatiently.

"I led the king," the old woman insisted.

"Let her take it back and lead the king, Bill," two onlookers pleaded.

"Not in this life," Frump snarled. "Your play, Minnie."

Minnie was unhappy with herself and more so with Frump. "Shame," she quavered, "taking advantage of my old eyes."

"Just play," said Frump, unabashed.

Minnie ruffed the third diamond and defiantly led a low trump. "Here, if you want tricks so much, have another."

The V.E. won and thought for a long time. He finally led another diamond — as good as anything — and Minnie ruffed with dummy's last trump and paused.

"She can draw trumps and run the clubs," I croaked, trying to keep my voice down. The kibitzers couldn't restrain themselves any longer and burst into excited babble, but Minnie's huddle lengthened.

"What is the woman thinking about?" Ed almost sobbed.

"She thinks the clubs are blocked!" I said in a panic. "She's wondering if she should take the spade finesse."

Ed rose and strode toward the table. "Your glasses need cleaning, Minnie," he said gently. "Let me do it." He plucked the aged bifocals off her nose and retired to the far end of the room.

Minnie peered through the mists toward dummy. "Now, what were your clubs, partner?"

"King, ten, six, four, deuce," Henrietta replied shakily.

Minnie squinted at her hand and then at dummy again. "Low club, please," she said firmly.

A few minutes later, Ed and I straggled out the club's big front door. A rainbow was apologizing for the day's angry sky.

"You know," I said, "I think it's time we offered Minnie lifetime free plays."

"First order of business," Ed agreed, "after we cancel the Perfect Game."

As a baseball announcer would have said, Bill Frump flirted with perfection. She just wouldn't flirt back.

PART the FOURTH

Sit Beside Me

In a Swiss Teams at a weekend Sectional, our opponents are good players. Both sides are vulnerable, and I'm South, in fourth position, with

♠ K
♥ K 10 8 4 2
♦ A J 4
♣ 7 6 5 4

West passes, my partner opens 1♣, I respond 1♥ and partner raises to 2♥.

The worth of my hand is unclear. There are plus features: I like the fifth trump and the "working" ♦J. There are minuses: the bare ♠K may be worthless, and the four low cards in the suit partner bid aren't encouraging.

I judge the hand worth an invitation to game. But since it's IMPs and we're vulnerable, the odds favor bidding game with significantly less than a 50% chance. I stand to gain 10 IMPs if 4♥ makes (+620 against +170 at the other table) but lose 6 IMPs if it fails (-100 against +140). That assumes no extra undertricks and no penalty double; neither is likely here.

Vulnerable at IMPs, my tendency with a sound invitation is to bid game. I stretch to invite game — I believe in aggressive invitations, else games will be missed — but not to accept. This approach avoids poor games when both partners are too aggressive. (I can understand the alternative approach — invite soundly, accept tentatively — which reduces the risk of going minus when partner rejects your invitation.)

When I leap to 4♥, everyone passes, and West leads the ♦5.

```
            ♠ Q 4 3 2
            ♥ A J 9 7
            ♦ 10 3
            ♣ A Q 3


            ♠ K
            ♥ K 10 8 4 2
            ♦ A J 4
            ♣ 7 6 5 4
```

WEST	NORTH	EAST	SOUTH
Pass	1♣	Pass	1♥
Pass	2♥	Pass	4♥
All Pass			

I play low from dummy, East puts up the queen and I win. Partner has nothing extra, but the contract looks worthwhile. I'll have no problem is the trumps come in, and I have a chance if they don't.

At the second trick I return a diamond. I can set up the ♦J for a club discard from dummy, and I'd like to know which defender has the ♦K. West takes the king and shifts to the ♣J. I doubt that can be a singleton; then West might have led it at trick one instead of a risky diamond. I finesse with the ♣Q and East plays low.

The contract looks safe. I can take the top trumps, and even if I run into a 4-0 break, I should lose at most one trump, a diamond and a spade. But since they'll probably bid this game at the other table, I don't mind trying to pick up an IMP by making an overtrick.

Still trying to place the cards, I lead to the ♠K next. West takes the ace and leads another club to dummy's ace. Now I can handle the trumps: I've seen West play the ♠A, ♣J and ♦K, and I know he has the ♣K. He passed as dealer, so East has the ♥Q.

124

```
              ♠ Q 4 3 2
              ♥ A J 9 7
              ♦ 10 3
              ♣ A Q 3
♠ A 9 5                      ♠ J 10 8 7 6
♥ 3                          ♥ Q 6 5
♦ K 7 6 5 2                  ♦ Q 9 8
♣ K J 10 2                   ♣ 9 8
              ♠ K
              ♥ K 10 8 4 2
              ♦ A J 4
              ♣ 7 6 5 4
```

I ruff a spade, discard dummy's low club on the ♦J, lead a trump to the ace and let the jack ride. West shows out, and I take the rest.

My guess at the other-table result was off target. They got to 4♥, but our West led the ♣J. South won the finesse but had no club discard coming on the ♦J. He mis-guessed the trumps, and the defense gave nothing away, so 4♥ failed.

If I'd taken ten tricks, we'd have gained 12 IMPs instead of 13. Players seldom worry about overtricks at IMPs, especially in a long match. If you risk a cold contract for an overtrick IMP and go down, you may be able to contend that your play would have gained points in the long run, but the adverse psychological effect on your team matters more. Moreover, the mental energy you spend chasing an overtrick may come in handy on a more important deal.

In a Swiss Teams, though, I don't look a gift overtrick in the mouth. Plenty of matches have been decided by gossamer-thin margins.

In a local Swiss Teams, I'm playing with a new partner. When we compared notes before the game, we took time to discuss "style" as well as system, and he told me he likes to open light, shapely hands. I promised to try to cope. In our first match, with only our side vulnerable, I hold

♠ 10 8 6 5
♥ K Q
♦ A Q 6 4
♣ A 6 5

My partner, North, deals and opens 1♣, and East doubles. I redouble, and after two passes, East rescues himself to 1♦.

At a different vulnerability, I might double that, following the odds. If we beat it only two tricks, we might lose a little; if we beat it three, we'd gain a little. But if a game happened to fail at the other table, we'd gain a lot. At this vulnerability, though, I can't afford to settle for +300 when we may be cold for +630 at 3NT. We might lose 8 IMPs.

I'm glad I have 15 points and not 11 or 12. When my hand is this strong and East has doubled, I suspect my partner is in there on one of his light openings. If my hand were slightly weaker, I'd have to guess whether to insist on game or invite.

Should I just bid 3NT or look for a better spot? I could cue-bid 2♦ or try 1♠—after my redouble, a new suit would be forcing—but even if partner has four spades, East may also have four for his double. How about a jump to 2NT? It would be forcing, I think, but partner might not agree, especially if he opened light. So I leap to 3NT. Maybe partner has a long club suit I can use.

Everyone passes, and West leads the ♦3.

♠ K 9 2
♥ A 7 5 3
♦ 2
♣ K J 7 4 3

♠ 10 8 6 5
♥ K Q
♦ A Q 6 4
♣ A 6 5

WEST	NORTH	EAST	SOUTH
	1♣	Dbl	Redbl
Pass	Pass	1♦	3NT
All Pass			

Light it is. I wouldn't have opened, but to each his own style.

East puts up the ♦K, and I take the ace. I can count two diamonds and three hearts, so only four clubs will see me home. Suppose I unblock the ♥KQ, take the ♣A and finesse with the ♣J. I'd cut myself off from my second diamond trick, but I might survive. If the ♣J won and East showed out, I could take the ♣K and concede a club. West, I expect, would shift to a spade, and East would win cheaply and exit with a heart to dummy. I'd take the ♥A, cash the good club and exit with a heart, and if East won, he'd have to give me my ninth trick in spades or diamonds.

That plan offers a chance for ten tricks but isn't safe for nine. If West happened to hold four hearts and four clubs, he'd get in twice for spade leads. Since it's IMPs, and making the contract is the goal, I play as safe as I can: I lead a club at the second trick, and when East plays the eight, I play low from dummy. The full deal is:

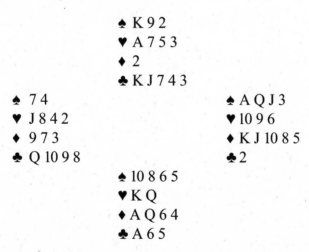

West shifts to a spade, and East wins with the jack and exits with a heart. I take the ♥KQ, the ♦Q and the ♣A, finesse with the ♣J and cash two more clubs.

West did have four hearts. Most Wests would have bid 1♥ over my redouble to suggest a place to play.

At the other table, North wasn't a light opener, but the East player on our team was: he started with 1♦ in second seat. After South and West passed, North reopened with a double, and South passed for penalty. That would have been a headhunting action even at a different vulnerability, and even though the defense managed eight tricks — three hearts, a spade, a club, South's two high trumps and an extra trump — for +300, we gained 7 IMPs.

In a local duplicate, our opponents are one of the better pairs in the club. Playing against experts is easier in a way because you can trust them to bid and play logically.

Both sides are vulnerable, and I'm South, the dealer, with

♠ A J
♥ K Q 9 8 3
♦ J 10 3
♣ A Q 4

I don't mind opening 1NT with a five-card major, but this hand is a little heavy. Our range is 15 to 17 points, but I also have the good five-card suit. So I open 1♥. If partner responds 1♠, I'll stretch slightly to rebid 2NT.

The opponents pass, and my partner raises to 2♥. Since his raise improves my hand, I'm worth at the least a try for game. Since I have plenty of losers, I'll settle for a try, and 2NT is the most descriptive try. If my partner's hand is also balanced, 3NT may be the only makable game.

My partner huddles and takes a card from his bidding box: 4♥. Everyone passes.

West ponders his lead. I expect a trump lead after the auction we had — North's preference for a suit contract suggests ruffing potential — but West comes forth with the ♠2.

♠ Q 3
♥ J 10 4
♦ A Q 9 2
♣ 10 5 3 2

♠ A J
♥ K Q 9 8 3
♦ J 10 3
♣ A Q 4

WEST	NORTH	EAST	SOUTH
			1♥
Pass	2♥	Pass	2NT
Pass	4♥	All Pass	

Our bidding isn't unreasonable, but I expect most pairs will land at 3NT. The auction at many tables will be 1NT-3NT. I need to win one more trick at hearts than the notrumpers win.

I put up the ♣Q — I'd like to know who has the king — and East covers. I take the ♣A and lead a trump to dummy, and East produces the ace and returns a spade. I take the jack and draw trumps, finding that West had 7-6-2.

The deal seems to be as good as over. I just have the minor-suit finesses to take. When I lead the ♦J, West plays the king. I win and return a diamond to my ten, and East discards a spade. On the ♦Q and ♦9 he discards a club and another spade, and I discard a club. Now I lead a club from dummy, and East follows low.

If the ♣K is onside, I can take 12 tricks for +680. The Souths at 3NT may also take 12 tricks, but I can't help that. I hope the ♣K is wrong. Then we may salvage a few matchpoints because some Souths at 3NT may try to make six and be held to four. I'm about to table my ♣Q, but I take a moment to reflect. Aside from the matchpoint considerations, do I have any excuse to decline the finesse?

Let me count West's hand. He had five diamonds and three trumps, and his opening lead of the ♠2 suggests four cards in that suit. So West had a singleton club, and he also had a weak hand. If I sat West with

♠ 10 8 4 2   ♥ 7 6 2   ♦ K 8 7 6 5   ♣ 7,

what would I have led?

I take back the ♣Q and replace it with the ace, and the full deal is

♠ Q 3
♥ J 10 4
♦ A Q 9 2
♣ 10 5 3 2

♠ 10 8 4 2	♠ K 9 7 6 5
♥ 7 6 2	♥ A 5
♦ K 8 7 6 5	♦ 4
♣ K	♣ J 9 8 7 6

♠ A J
♥ K Q 9 8 3
♦ J 10 3
♣ A Q 4

Players love to lead singletons, but not singleton kings.

This was a lucky deal for us since the lie of the cards made our doubtful contract a winner. Not one of the pairs at 3NT took 12 tricks.

In a Sectional Open Pairs, neither side is vulnerable, and I'm South, in fourth position, with

♠ K J 9
♥ A 6 5
♦ A J 4 3
♣ J 5 2

I hear three passes and open 1♦, and my partner responds 1♥.

I'm a believer in raising a major-suit response (particularly a 1♠ response) on three-card support with any excuse, but here I can see none. This is a textbook 1NT rebid. To my mild surprise, everyone passes, and West leads the ♠7.

♠ 6 5 3
♥ K 4 3 2
♦ K 10 6 2
♣ K 4

♠ K J 9
♥ A 6 5
♦ A J 4 3
♣ J 5 2

WEST	NORTH	EAST	SOUTH
Pass	Pass	Pass	1♦
Pass	1♥	Pass	1NT
All Pass			

At IMPs, North might have taken a 2♦ preference, trying to play in a contract most likely to produce a plus. At matchpoints, where we need a large plus, he took his chances at 1NT. If I can win eight tricks for +120, I'll beat pairs who are +110 at diamonds.

East takes the ♠A and returns the deuce. I try the jack without much hope, and West's queen wins. I await the third spade, but instead West huddles and squirms and shifts to the ♥J. I'm sure he had five spades; how come he didn't establish his suit?

Only one answer makes sense: West doesn't have a sure entry. So East has the ♣A, the ♥Q and the ♠A. He didn't open the bidding in third position, so I can place West with both minor-suit queens.

I take the ♥A, cash the ♦A and lead a diamond. West's queen comes up, and dummy's king wins. Next I lead a low heart. East puts up the queen and exits with a diamond, and I cash two diamonds and take the ♥K. If East started with 2-4-3-4 distribution, I'll throw him in with the fourth heart and force him to give dummy the ♣K; but the hearts break 3-3, so I have eight tricks without an endplay and score +120. The full deal:

```
              ♠ 6 5 3
              ♥ K 4 3 2
              ♦ K 10 6 2
              ♣ K 4
♠ Q 10 8 7 4                    ♠ A 2
♥ J 10 7                        ♥ Q 9 8
♦ Q 7                           ♦ 9 8 5
♣ Q 6 3                         ♣ A 10 9 8 7
              ♠ K J 9
              ♥ A 6 5
              ♦ A J 4 3
              ♣ J 5 2
```

We scored well in the matchpoint column. One or two North-Souths managed nine tricks at notrump, obviously with help, but many pairs played at diamonds. They had two spades and a heart to lose, and even when declarer got the diamonds right and brought off an endplay to avoid a second club loser, he took only nine tricks.

At my table, West would have done better to continue spades at the third trick, entry or no entry.

****

132

As I See It

Cue-bidding Style

Twenty years ago, when I analyzed the U.S. vs. Austria Olympiad Open Teams final for the 1988 World Championship Book, I had to comment on this result:

WEST	EAST
♠ 10 9 7 5 3	♠ Q
♥ A 10 9 8 7	♥ 6 5
♦ A K	♦ 6 4
♣ 9	♣ A K Q J 10 7 5 4

1♠	2♣
2♥	4♣
4♦	6♣

East-West were great players, but their slam had no play. I wrote that they apparently had no answer to a question any aspiring partnership must address: in a slam auction, are cue-bids under game constructive or cooperative? Must a player cue-bid despite no extra values or may he decline? East's 4♣ was forcing, and West thought he had to cue-bid 4♦ despite his minimum, But if that was the partnership style, East's leap to 6♣ was unjustified.

I fear that in 2008 most experts would feel obliged to bid 4♦, but in my opinion that style dilutes the major advantage of cue-bidding: the opportunity for either player to use his judgment.

An internet deal I watched did nothing to change my mind.

Dlr: North
Vul: N-S
IMPs

```
                    ♠ K 9 8 7
                    ♥ Q J 4
                    ♦ A K J 5 2
                    ♣ 8
♠ 4                                 ♠ Q 5 2
♥ A K 9 5                           ♥ 10 7 6 3
♦ 9 7 3                             ♦ Q 10 8 6
♣ 10 9 7 5 3                        ♣ J 2
                    ♠ A J 10 6 3
                    ♥ 8 2
                    ♦ 4
                    ♣ A K Q 6 4
```

WEST	NORTH	EAST	SOUTH
	1♦	Pass	1♠
Pass	3♠	Pass	4♣
Pass	4♦	Pass	5♣
Pass	5♠	All Pass	

West cashed his high hearts, and South failed to pick up East's ♠Q, so the result was down one.

This was in an expert game with many spectators, and the comments came quickly. One spec insisted that South's first cue-bid should have been 4♦, not 4♣. The idea was that South was worried solely about hearts, hence he should have cue-bid in a way that would force North to show a heart control if he had one. It was an imaginative idea, but other specs called it nonsense. The majority view seemed to be that South's second try of 5♣ was too bold.

Nobody commented on North's bidding, so I suspect I was alone in putting the blame on him. I suppose North's raise to 3♠ was defensible — he was really worth about 2.75♠ — but if I raised to 3♠ with that hand, I wouldn't cooperate in a slam hunt. Over 4♣, North should have signed off at 4♠.

It's all very well to say that North has an "automatic" cue-bid of 4♦, but he has a dead minimum in high cards and non-slam values. It's all very well to say that North's 4♦ promises no extra values, but human nature being what it is, South will be more apt to get excited when he hears North cue-bid. It's a wonder that instead of bidding 5♣, South didn't try 5♠, insisting on slam if North had a heart control.

What would have happened if North had signed off? Maybe South would have tried again with 5♣ anyway, but I doubt that any Souths would have passed 4♠ on the actual auction.

Discuss cue-bidding style with your partner. My advice is to avoid a style that's inflexible.

Stay with Happiness

You're North, playing IMPs on the internet. With only your side vulnerable, you hold

♠ 9 5
♥ —
♦ K Q 6 5 4 3 2
♣ K 7 5 2

WEST	NORTH	EAST	SOUTH
		2♥ (1)	2♠
4♥	?		

(1) weak

What is your call?

In one of my first events as a tournament player, I opposed a pro and his client. My partner and I bid tentatively to an ill-judged 4♠ contract, and the client, who had a trump stack, doubled. My partner, who had been mentally squirming throughout the auction, scrambled out to 4NT. Everyone passed, and he went down one. The original 4♠ would have been down at least four.

"When they were at 4♠," the pro told his client patiently, "you were happy. Stay with happiness."

Doubling the only contract you can beat is supposed to be a classic bidding error, but some doubles are worse than others. I was watching an all-expert IMP game — North was a multiple world champion — when this deal appeared.

```
Dlr: East              ♠ 9 5
Vul: N-S               ♥ —
IMPs                   ♦ K Q 6 5 4 3 2
                       ♣ K 7 5 2
         ♠ A J 3 2                        ♠ 8 6
         ♥ 10 9 6 3                       ♥ A K J 7 5 4
         ♦ —                              ♦ J 8 7
         ♣ 10 9 8 4 3                     ♣ J 6
                       ♠ K Q 10 7 4
                       ♥ Q 8 2
                       ♦ A 10 9
                       ♣ A Q
```

WEST	NORTH	EAST	SOUTH
		2♥	2♠
4♥	4♠(!)	Pass	Pass
Dbl	5♦	All Pass	

West's double of 4♠ was a howler. He couldn't be sure of beating any alternative game – or of beating 4♠. (Do you think North risked 4♠ because he thought he'd get doubled if he couldn't make it?) North would have made 6♦ if he'd been there, but South, who was no doubt delighted to hear North's 5♦, stayed with happiness. It was hard for him to bid a slam when he'd been doubled at game.

At 5♦ North played safe for 11 tricks and made 12 anyway when the defense slipped.

What would have happened at 4♠ undoubled? I can't say, but here's a possible result after a heart opening lead. South ruffs, takes the ♣AQ, ruffs a heart and leads the ♣K. East ruffs, and South throws his last heart. He ruffs the heart return and leads the ♠K, ducked. South can then escape for down one by abandoning trumps, losing three trumps to West but keeping control. If instead South goes for broke and leads another trump, he loses control and goes down three. (A trump opening lead would always hold South to eight tricks.)

I know many good players who double freely and dare the opponents to run. They figure two things must happen for the double to backfire: the opponents must have a better spot and must find it. Nevertheless, consider carefully before you double. Nobody ever went broke by taking a profit.

Dodos and Doubles

Take this five-problem quiz. IMP scoring.

(1) Neither side vulnerable. You hold

♠ 3   ♥ 10 6   ♦ A K 10 9 8 5   ♣ A K Q 8.

As dealer you open 1♦. Your partner responds 1♥, RHO overcalls 1♠, you bid 2♣ and LHO jumps to 3♠ (preemptive). Your partner doubles, and RHO passes. What is your call?

(2) Neither side vulnerable. You hold

♠ A J 6 5 2   ♥ Q J 8   ♦ K Q 4 3   ♣ A.

As dealer you open 1♠. Your partner raises to 2♠ and RHO jumps to 4♦. What is your call?

(3) Neither side vulnerable. You hold

♠ A   ♥ 9 8   ♦ A 10 4   ♣ J 9 6 5 4 3 2.

The dealer, at your left, passes and your partner opens 1♠. RHO overcalls 2♥, and you try a negative double. LHO jumps to 4♥, and two passes follow. What is your call?

(4) Your side is vulnerable. You hold

♠ K J 9 8 2   ♥ A 5 4   ♦ 5 4 3   ♣ J 6.

After three passes, your partner opens 1♦. RHO overcalls 1♥, you bid 1♠, LHO lifts to 2♥ and your partner rebids 3♦, RHO competes with 3♥. What is your call?

(5) Both sides vulnerable. You hold

♠ 7 3   ♥ K 7 6   ♦ A K J   ♣ J 10 8 6 4.

Your partner deals and opens 1♠, and RHO jumps to 5♦. What is your call?

Recently I wrote up this deal for my syndicated column:

```
Dlr: East              ♠ 10 9 5 4
Vul: Both              ♥ 10 8 7 6 2
                       ♦ Q J
                       ♣ 5 3
    ♠ 8                                ♠ A Q 7 6 3 2
    ♥ A Q J 4                          ♥ 9 3
    ♦ K 8 7 5 2                        ♦ A 6 3
    ♣ J 7 4                            ♣ A 6
                       ♠ K J
                       ♥ K 5
                       ♦ 10 9 4
                       ♣ K Q 10 9 8 2
```

WEST   NORTH   EAST   SOUTH
                       1♠   2♣
Dbl (1)   All Pass

(1) For penalty, vintage 50 years ago

West speculated with a double, seeing a profit on defense if East could sit for it. Since East had a good defensive hand, he was happy to accept the suggestion.

They picked declarer clean: spade opening lead to the ace; heart shift to the king and ace; ♥Q; ♥J ruffed by South as East shed a diamond; ♣K to the ace; spade ruff; ♦A; ♦K; third diamond with East overruffing dummy; spade to promote West's ♣J. Down four.

My column was a lament. We seldom see such results nowadays — the product of good and bad judgment in the auction — because progress in bidding theory has given us the negative double. In 2008 West would double or bid 2♦ at his first turn, and even if he passed and East reopened with a double instead of with 2♠, West couldn't make a unilateral decision to play for penalty.

Nowadays every double you hear has some arcane meaning. The penalty double, I fear, is going the way of the dodo and the passenger pigeon. The double has become a sheep in sheep's clothing. Opponents can bid with impunity.

In an allegedly strong internet game, I watched three consecutive deals that I found mystifying.

		♠ 9 8 5 2	
Dlr: West		♥ 9 8 7 2	
Vul: None		♦ 4	
		♣ J 7 6 4	

♠ 3		♠ K Q 7 6
♥ 10 6		♥ A K 5 4
♦ A K 10 9 8 5		♦ 7 6 3
♣ A K Q 8		♣ 10 3

	♠ A J 10 4	
	♥ Q J 3	
	♦ Q J 2	
	♣ 9 5 2	

WEST	NORTH	EAST	SOUTH
1♦	Pass	1♥	1♠ (1)
2♣	3♠	Dbl	Pass
?			

(1) Good grief!

I was trying to calculate the upcoming penalty (and was delighted to see that South was about to get what was coming to him) when West ... bid 5♦! All passed, and the defense got a spade and a trump, +400 to East-West.

West explained that he thought East's double simply showed values but no clear bid.

		♠ A J 6 5 2	
Dlr: North		♥ Q J 8	
Vul: None		♦ K Q 4 3	
		♣ A	

♠ 9		♠ K 10 7 3
♥ 2		♥ A 7 5 4 3
♦ J 10 8 7 6 5 2		♦ —
♣ K Q 10 4		♣ J 8 5 3

	♠ Q 8 4	
	♥ K 10 9 6	
	♦ A 9	
	♣ 9 7 6 2	

WEST	NORTH	EAST	SOUTH
	1♠	Pass	2♠
4♦	4♠ (1)	All Pass	

(1) Holy guacamole!

North could have taken a sure profit — which would have been +500 — by doubling 4♦. He made 4♠, off two trumps and a heart, but if the ♠Q and ♠3 were swapped, 4♠ would have been down two and 4♦ would still be down three. (East-West could have beaten 4♠ on the actual deal.)

One wonders if North wanted ♦AQ108 to double 4♦. Could the modern preoccupation with competitive doubles be having an unhealthy side-effect? Are players forgetting that they might punish an opponent who puts his neck on the chopping block?

```
Dlr: North          ♠ J 5 3
Vul: E-W            ♥ J 10 7 6 4
                    ♦ J 9 6 3
                    ♣ A
    ♠ A                          ♠ K Q 9 8 7
    ♥ 9 8                        ♥ 5 3
    ♦ A 10 4                     ♦ K Q 7
    ♣ J 9 6 5 4 3 2              ♣ Q 10 8
                    ♠ 10 6 4 2
                    ♥ A K Q 2
                    ♦ 8 5 2
                    ♣ K 7
```

WEST	NORTH	EAST	SOUTH
	Pass	1♠	2♥ (1)
Dbl	4♥	Pass	Pass
5♣ (2)	All Pass		

(1) Perhaps carried away by his success on the first deal
(2) Arrggh!

This time West had two aces, including the singleton ace of his partner's bid suit, and two fast heart losers, but he still wouldn't double. His 5♣ went down two when 4♥ would have been down three.

Quiz problem (4) appeared in The Bridge World's Master Solvers Club. Your side is vulnerable. You hold

♠ K J 9 8 2 ♥ A 5 4 ♦ 5 4 3 ♣ J 6.

After three passes, your partner opens 1♦. RHO overcalls 1♥, you bid 1♠, LHO lifts to 2♥ and your partner rebids 3♦, RHO competes with 3♥. What is your call?

Most of the panel voted for 4♦, pass (an action the Law of Total Tricks would support) or 3NT. But a couple of experts thought the correct action was double—after which, no doubt, they expected their partner to know their exact strength and pattern. That was in 1996; I fear there might be more than two doublers now. (Do you ever ponder, as I do, that pairs who use these all-purpose doubles must face constant ethical problems? Maybe an experienced world-class pair can make such doubles in tempo, but can lesser mortals?)

I can see it now. In the next millennium, an archaeologist excavating a site finds a tattered copy of a bridge magazine with a description of a deal played at 4♠ doubled. He is bemused. "Do you suppose," he mutters, "that a double was once used to increase the size of a penalty?"

This was the quiz problem (5):

Both sides vulnerable. You hold

♠ 7 3 ♥ K 7 6 ♦ A K J ♣ J 10 8 6 4.

Your partner deals and opens 1♠, and RHO jumps to 5♦. What is your call?

Let's hope that 100 years from now, a player will be able to double, and he won't have to fear that his partner will interpret it as a hair-splitting, "card-showing," you-figure-it-out action.

****

At My Club

Dlr: South   ♠ Q J 2
Vul: N-S   ♥ Q 10 8
             ♦ Q 7
             ♣ J 8 5 3 2

	♠ K 10 3		♠ 9 7 6 4
	♥ A 7 3		♥ K J 6
	♦ J 10 9 8		♦ 6 5 4 2
	♣ 10 7 4		♣ A 9

             ♠ A 8 5
             ♥ 9 5 4 2
             ♦ A K 3
             ♣ K Q 6

WEST	NORTH	EAST	SOUTH
			1NT
Pass	2NT	Pass	3NT
All Pass			

You can ask Wendy, my club's feminist, how many sensitive, caring, unselfish men it takes to wash the dishes, and she'll say both of them.

"Don't you believe men have any redeeming virtues at all?" I asked her.

"Men are like copiers," Wendy replied, "good for reproduction and not much else."

I was watching when Wendy cut her adversary Cy the Cynic, a shameless chauvinist, in a money game. Cy, West, led the ♦J against 3NT, and South won with the king and led the ♣K. Wendy took her ace and fired back a diamond, won by dummy's queen.

Declarer next let the ♠Q ride. Cy took the king and produced—really, reproduced—another diamond, and South took four clubs, three diamonds and two spades.

"Call the copier repairperson," Wendy growled.

Cy had a paper jam when he led the third diamond. At that point he could place South with 16 points: ♣KQ, ♦AK, ♠A. Hence South couldn't have the ♥K, and if he had the jack, the defenders had no chance. Cy must shift to the ♥A and a low heart, and East-West will get the five tricks they are due.

****

Sit Beside Me

In a local Knockout Teams, both sides are vulnerable, and as the dealer I pick up

```
♠ —
♥ 9 6 4 3
♦ 8 4
♣ A K 9 8 7 5 2
```

Time to preempt, I imagine, but this is not a textbook 3♣ opening. The hand contains two Quick Tricks plus four cards in a major suit.

I'm not so worried about the heart support. If partner has hearts, the opponents surely have a spade fit, and the deal won't belong to us unless partner's hand is strong enough to act over 3♣. (At least, that's what I intend to tell him if I play at 3♣ when we're cold for 5♥.) The defensive tricks worry me more, but few players need a perfect hand to preempt. If you wait to sail until every danger is past, you'll never leave port.

When I open 3♣, West passes, and North ponders and raises to 5♣. Everyone passes, so he must have bid it to make. West leads a trump, which doesn't please me when I see dummy.

```
♠ 10 8 5 3
♥ A 5 2
♦ A K 6
♣ Q J 10

♠ —
♥ 9 6 4 3
♦ 8 4
♣ A K 9 8 7 5 2
```

WEST	NORTH	EAST	SOUTH
			3♣
Pass	5♣	All Pass	

The ♣Q wins, but East discards the ♦J. The contract would be a claimer if trumps broke 2-1, but now I have to worry about my fourth heart. If West gets in twice with heart tricks, he'll lead a trump each time, and then if hearts don't break 3-3, my fourth heart will be a loser.

Luckily, I see a way to counter West's good lead. I ruff a spade at the second trick, lead a diamond to dummy, ruff a spade, get back with a diamond and ruff a third spade with the ♣A. I return a trump to dummy to ruff the last spade, go back to the ♥A and ruff dummy's low diamond. I have ten tricks in the bag, and dummy still has a trump. The full deal:

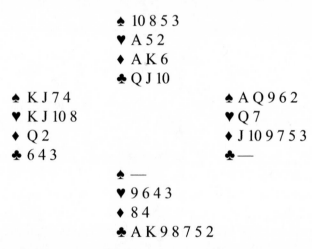

```
                    ♠ 10 8 5 3
                    ♥ A 5 2
                    ♦ A K 6
                    ♣ Q J 10
  ♠ K J 7 4                        ♠ A Q 9 6 2
  ♥ K J 10 8                       ♥ Q 7
  ♦ Q 2                            ♦ J 10 9 7 5 3
  ♣ 6 4 3                          ♣ —
                    ♠ —
                    ♥ 9 6 4 3
                    ♦ 8 4
                    ♣ A K 9 8 7 5 2
```

I hoped for a swing: I thought if South opened 3♣ at the other table, North might try 3NT and go down on a spade lead.

We won a swing, but not as I expected. In the replay South preferred a stodgy first-seat pass. After West passed, North opened 1♦ in his stronger three-card minor. East overcalled 1♠, South bid 2♣ and West jumped to 3♠ (limit). North passed when he might have supported with 4♣, and when East went on to 4♠, seduced by the lure of the vulnerable game bonus, South couldn't act, and North judged to defend because of his four trumps.

It seemed a forcing defense would trouble 4♠. South led the ♣K. East ruffed, led a diamond to the queen and king, ruffed the club return and

146

forced out the ♦A. East ruffed the next club, cashed the ♠AQ and then judged well to take the ♦J and lead the ♥Q. North ducked, but when he won the next heart, he had to put dummy in to draw trumps and take the rest. Making four, +620, and 15 IMPs to us.

My team fractured the Law of Total Tricks in this deal. The "Law" allotted our side 19 tricks with our 19 trumps, so both 5♣ and 4♠ might have been down one. The Law was off by one trick per table. We actually took 21 tricks. Well, what's one trick among friends?

In a Regional Swiss Teams, my team isn't the strongest in the room and is comfortably out of contention for the big prize. Our record is 5 and 2. Still, if we win our last match, we'll crack the overall awards. The first two boards are uneventful, and then as South, with both sides vulnerable, I hold

♠ J 4
♥ K J 9 8 7 6
♦ 10 5
♣ A K J

East, the dealer, passes, and I open 1♥. West passes, and my partner raises to 2♥. East then backs in with a double.

Clearly, I can compete to the three level. I'm never sure in these situations whether to bid 3♥ directly or wait. The danger in bidding directly is that East-West may even be cold for 4♠, and my bid may push them into it; if West competes with 3♠, East may go on. I doubt that will happen here when I have at least two defensive tricks in clubs plus some other values. Maybe if I bid 3♥ right away, I'll keep West out, so I choose that action.

West duly passes, but my partner unexpectedly starts to think. Oh my. I hope he's doesn't think I have a good hand. If I were interested in game, I'd have redoubled or bid a new suit. After a while, though, North bids 4♥, and I'm afraid we just converted a plus to a minus.

Everyone passes, and West leads the ♦3.

                        ♠ A 10 3 2
                        ♥ A 10 5
                        ♦ 7 6
                        ♣ 8 4 3 2

                        ♠ J 4
                        ♥ K J 9 8 7 6
                        ♦ 10 5
                        ♣ A K J

WEST	NORTH	EAST	SOUTH
		Pass	1♥
Pass	2♥	Dbl	3♥
Pass	4♥	All Pass	

I don't like it. Even if I pick up the trumps, I may have two black-suit losers. No doubt partner will explain later where he got his 4♥ bid. Meanwhile, I must do what I can with the contract.

East takes the ♦KA and shifts to the ♣5. I think I can place the cards. East didn't open but has shown the ♦AKJ (West would have led the ♦Q if he had Q-J). I'm also sure East has a spade honor: if West had the ♠KQ, he'd have led the ♠K instead of a diamond from a broken suit. Since East's double also suggests a distributional hand, I'm inclined to place West with the ♥Q and the ♣Q.

I take the ♣A and let the ♥J ride. If West has Q-4-3-2, I can't afford to cash the king first. East follows with the deuce, so I continue with the ♥K. East discards a diamond.

I think to lead the ♠J next is safe. West covers with the king, and I take the ace and lead the ♠10 to locate the queen for sure. East wins and leads a third spade, and I ruff and take the ♥A.

I'm sure West has the ♣Q. Not many Easts would have passed with

♠ Q 9 8 7   ♥ 2   ♦ A K J 4   ♣ Q 7 6 5.

I lead a club to my king, and luckily, the queen falls. I can claim the rest. The full deal:

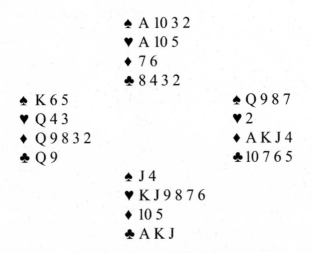

```
              ♠ A 10 3 2
              ♥ A 10 5
              ♦ 7 6
              ♣ 8 4 3 2
♠ K 6 5                      ♠ Q 9 8 7
♥ Q 4 3                      ♥ 2
♦ Q 9 8 3 2                  ♦ A K J 4
♣ Q 9                        ♣ 10 7 6 5
              ♠ J 4
              ♥ K J 9 8 7 6
              ♦ 10 5
              ♣ A K J
```

At the other table, East-West were playing a style that required them to open anything remotely resembling an opening bid. (That may help explain why our team didn't win this event.) East opened 1♦, South overcalled 1♥, West leaped to 3♦ (limit), North competed with 3♥ and South went on to 4♥. After a diamond lead, declarer mis-guessed everything and went down two, giving us a 13-IMP gain.

When we compared scores, our East-West credited the swing to their system, of course.

In an Open Pairs, both sides are vulnerable, and as dealer I pick up a hand that would hold promise for any matchpoint player.

```
              ♠ K
              ♥ J 4
              ♦ A 8 3
              ♣ A K Q 10 7 5 2
```

This is a Gambling 3NT opening in the style of some players, but my style is to open 3NT with a solid minor suit and nothing else. If opener may have side values, responder may be obliged to guess at the right contract. I start with 1♣.

149

West overcalls 1♠, and two passes follow. Now I can't do less than bid 3NT. My partner probably has a few values, and West, I trust, won't lay down the ♠A on opening lead. If he underleads, as most would, I'll have my nine tricks.

Everyone passes, and West doesn't choose his lead right away. I silently will him to lead a low spade. Eventually, the ♠7 appears — a pleasant sight — and the dummy is suitable.

```
              ♠ 10 8 4
              ♥ A 9 6 5 2
              ♦ Q 7 4
              ♣ 4 3

              ♠ K
              ♥ J 4
              ♦ A 8 3
              ♣ A K Q 10 7 5 2
```

WEST	NORTH	EAST	SOUTH
			1♣
1♠	Pass	Pass	3NT
All Pass			

I play the ♣8 from dummy, East contributes the jack and I win, trying not to look relieved. The deal isn't over. I'm safe for ten tricks, but I must try for more. For all I know, what has happened so far at my table may happen at others. To get a top, I'll need +660.

I peel off seven rounds of clubs. West, who had a low singleton, discards two diamonds, then three spades, then the ♥10. East has to find four pitches and lets go a low diamond, a middle heart, a spade and the ♦9. The position is

```
              ♠ 10
              ♥ A 9
              ♦ Q 7
              ♣

              ♠
              ♥ J 4
              ♦ A 8 3
              ♣
```

I next lead to the ♥A, and West plays the king. East follows with a heart lower than the one he'd discarded.

West must have had a six-card spade suit. East threw one spade but not two, so he probably began with three. If West still has the ♥Q left and has bared the ♦K, East's discards have been odd. My experience is that defenders don't discard diabolically; they try to send partner honest information. With three low hearts, East might have thrown all his hearts, and if West had ♥KQ10, he might have pitched his ♥10 early.

I'm willing to trust my reading of the deal: West is down to the ♠AQ and the guarded ♦K. So I lead a spade from dummy, and after West takes two spades, he must lead from the ♦K, and I make two overtricks. The full deal:

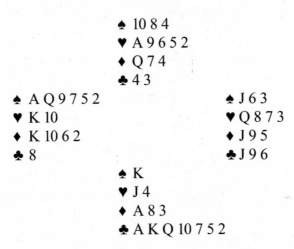

```
              ♠ 10 8 4
              ♥ A 9 6 5 2
              ♦ Q 7 4
              ♣ 4 3
♠ A Q 9 7 5 2              ♠ J 6 3
♥ K 10                    ♥ Q 8 7 3
♦ K 10 6 2                ♦ J 9 5
♣ 8                       ♣ J 9 6
              ♠ K
              ♥ J 4
              ♦ A 8 3
              ♣ A K Q 10 7 5 2
```

West reproached himself for his opening lead. Many players would have done the same, but perhaps West should have led the ♠A. When his hand was so strong, East was likely to play no part in the defense. Keeping communication by leading low wasn't necessary.

More questionable was East's play of the ♠J. If West's seven was fourth highest, I held only one higher spade, and East couldn't gain by squandering the jack. If he plays low, I can never take more than ten tricks.

I'm playing in a one-session pairs event with another partner who been swept up in the flood of light opening bids. That makes me uneasy as usual. As responder, I'm never sure whether to force to game when I have a 12-count.

As South, with only our side vulnerable, I hold

♠ Q 9 6 2
♥ Q 10 4
♦ K Q 9
♣ K 6 4

West, the dealer, passes, and my partner opens 1♣. East overcalls 1♦.

I suppose I should stick to the party line and respond 1♠. If partner raises to 2♠ or rebids 2♣, I'll try 3NT. I have only 12 points, but my diamond honors are well placed — my K-Q will be worth two tricks as if they were an A-K — and since partner has opened in a minor suit, maybe for once he'll have sound values.

Actually, I don't mind suppressing my spade suit. I can't jump to 2NT because that bid would be invitational, but I can bid 3NT. To mention the spades would be wrong if North has a hand such as

♥ K 5 4 3   ♥ K J 2   ♦ 6   ♣ A Q 10 8 3.

He'd never let me play 3NT, and 4♠ might fail when 3NT will make. Of course, North could have a hand where 4♠ or a partscore is better, so I'm masterminding a bit, but at least it's matchpoints: I have much to gain, and if my action turns out badly, I'll have to justify it only to my partner and not to teammates.

When I bid 3NT, everyone passes and West leads the ♦10. North proudly tables his dummy.

♠ 3
♥ A J 6 3
♦ 6 3
♣ A J 10 7 5 2

♠ Q 9 6 2
♥ Q 10 4
♦ K Q 9
♣ K 6 4

WEST	NORTH	EAST	SOUTH
Pass	1♣	1♦	3NT
All Pass			

I'd be willing to open the North hand if the long suit were a major, but even then the hand would seem more like a sound weak two-bid to me. Light openings have advantages, but constructive bidding is difficult when the range for an opening bid is wide.

Meanwhile, I've gotten us into a miserable contract. No game is attractive. We really belong at a club partial, though I can't see how we could stop low once North opened and East overcalled.

East puts up the ♦A, and since I'm praying for a diamond continuation instead of a spade shift, I drop my queen. It's a dusty ploy, but I lose nothing by trying it. Sure enough, East returns a diamond, and my nine wins. West looks annoyed.

Now I have nine tricks if I can bring in the clubs, but I can delay that guess. First I lead the ♥Q. If West plays low smoothly, I'll take the ace and try the clubs, but West actually covers with the ♥K. When I cash three hearts, both defenders follow, so I take the 13th heart. East discards a diamond and West a spade.

I come back to the ♣K, both defenders playing low, and take my ♦K. West throws another spade. When I lead another club, West plays low. It's time to guess.

I know West started with three hearts and two diamonds, and I suspect he had one of the top spade honors. If East had both, he might have cashed one at the second trick to see his partner's reaction. If I go up with the ♣A, I'm playing West for a hand such as

♠ K J 8 7 5 4 ♥ K 9 5 ♦ 10 4 ♣ 8 3.

That looks like a possible weak two-bid at favorable vulnerability, so I finesse with the ♣J. The full deal:

```
                          ♠ 3
                          ♥ A J 6 3
                          ♦ 6 3
                          ♣ A J 10 7 5 2
        ♠ K 10 8 5 4                      ♠ A J 7
        ♥ K 9 5                           ♥ 8 7 2
        ♦ 10 4                            ♦ A J 8 7 5 2
        ♣ Q 8 3                           ♣ 9
                          ♠ Q 9 6 2
                          ♥ Q 10 4
                          ♦ K Q 9
                          ♣ K 6 4
```

East, as his partner is quick to inform him, would have done better to shift to the ♠J at the second trick.

****

As I See It

One Little Trump

"It's a mistake to act because there isn't time to think. Time given to thought is the greatest of all time savers."—quote from Alfred Sheinwold's archives.

I have no statistics to prove it, but I'd bet the average time that internet players spend on a deal is less than the eight minutes allotted in tournaments. Many of the games are casual, with pick-up partnerships, and often a player may be grabbing a few minutes to enjoy himself. Players may feel they mustn't impose on their fellow players by taking a long time over a difficult problem in bidding or play.

Courtesy and consideration are admirable, of course, but rushing is a bad habit to acquire. I was watching an IMP game with four capable players when this deal appeared:

```
Dlr: East        ♠ A Q 7 2
Vul: Both        ♥ A Q 6
                 ♦ 7
                 ♣ A Q 10 9 5
    ♠ 5                        ♠ 8 6 4
    ♥ K J 10 8 4               ♥ 7 3
    ♦ K 9 5 4 2               ♦ 8 6 3
    ♣ 8 3                     ♣ K J 6 4 2
                 ♠ K J 10 9 3
                 ♥ 9 5 2
                 ♦ A Q J 10
                 ♣ 7
```

WEST	NORTH	EAST	SOUTH
		Pass	1♠
Pass	2♣	Pass	2♦
Pass	3♠	Pass	4♠
Pass	4NT	Pass	5♥
Pass	6♠	All Pass	

North's bidding looks like a time-saver. His 4NT was Key Card Blackwood, and South's 5♥ showed the ♠K and ♦A. North then placed the contract, but presumably the auction would have been the same if South had held, say,

♠ K J 10 9 3   ♥ K 5 2   ♦ A Q J 10   ♣ 7.

West led the ♥J, and South got off on the wrong foot by taking the ace. It seems he might have tried the queen since West had merely led the unbid suit, and the danger of a ruff was minimal. Even so, South was safe if he guessed the diamonds. First, however, he thought he could afford a round of trumps. He cashed the ♠A ... and darkness descended.

South next took the ♦A and let the ♦Q ride, pitching a heart from dummy. He cashed the ♠10 and, when West discarded, led the ♦J. This time West covered with the king, and South pitched dummy's last heart, the queen. West then led a fourth diamond, South threw a club from dummy and East ruffed to beat the slam.

It wouldn't seem that drawing one little trump would be dangerous, but that's like saying the guillotine isn't dangerous because it cuts off only one head. Once South took the ♠A, intending to discard dummy's hearts on the diamonds, he could succeed only with the unlikely play of taking a double ruffing finesse in clubs. South would be safe if he drew one trump with his king and then guessed the diamonds, but I suspect his best approach was to start by drawing no trumps at all. He could get home with a crossruff.

The play, incidentally, took less time than you needed to read about it. It would have taken longer in a Vanderbilt match.

Rushing is a bad habit to acquire. Take your time. Save "lightning" games for chess. I never saw a really good bridge player who begrudged an opponent extra time on a tough deal.

When They Save

Try these three opening lead problems. Assume IMP scoring.

1. WEST	NORTH	EAST	SOUTH
1♠	Dbl	Redbl	2♦
Pass	3♦	3♠	4♦
4♠	5♦	Dbl	All Pass

East-West vulnerable. What should West lead from

♠ A Q 10 6 4   ♥ K 7 3   ♦ A 5 2   ♣ J 4 ?

2. WEST	NORTH	EAST	SOUTH
	Pass	Pass	Pass
1♠	Dbl	3♠	4♣
4♠	5♣	Pass	Pass
Dbl	All Pass		

Both sides vulnerable. What should West lead from

♠ K 10 9 6 4   ♥ A Q J   ♦ A K 4   ♣ 7 4 ?

3. WEST	NORTH	EAST	SOUTH
			2♥
Dbl	4♥	4♠	Pass
Pass	5♥	Pass	Pass
Dbl	All Pass		

North-South vulnerable. What should West lead from

♠ 9 7 5 4   ♥ J   ♦ A J 10 6 4   ♣ A K 8 ?

When the opponents sacrifice against your game, they'll have shape to compensate for their lack of high-card values. Since preventing declarer from scoring extra trump tricks may be the defenders' only pressing concern, a trump opening lead may be best.

Dlr: West   ♠ 7
Vul: E-W   ♥ A 10 5 4
                ♦ K J 6 3
                ♣ A 7 6 3

     ♠ A Q 10 6 4   ♠ K J 3
     ♥ K 7 3   ♥ Q J 9 6
     ♦ A 5 2   ♦ 7
     ♣ J 4   ♣ Q 10 9 5 2

                ♠ 9 8 5 2
                ♥ 8 2
                ♦ Q 10 9 8 4
                ♣ K 8

WEST	NORTH	EAST	SOUTH
1♠	Dbl	Redbl	2♦
Pass	3♦	3♠	4♦
4♠	5♦	Dbl	All Pass

West knows from East's redouble that East-West have most of the high cards. North-South are clearly sacrificing. So West should lead a low trump or the ace and another trump. When he gets back in, he can continue trumps, holding South to one spade ruff in dummy, and the result will be down three. If instead West leads the ♠A to get a peek at dummy, his trump shift will be too late to prevent declarer from ruffing two spades and escaping for down two. (South's sacrifice, as it happens, is a phantom.)

Dlr: North   ♠ A
Vul: Both   ♥ K 8 6
                ♦ Q 10 7 5 3
                ♣ K 9 6 3

     ♠ K 10 9 6 4   ♠ Q 8 7 3
     ♥ A Q J   ♥ 9 5 4 3
     ♦ A K 4   ♦ J 9 8 6
     ♣ 7 4   ♣ Q

                ♠ J 5 2
                ♥ 10 7 2
                ♦ 2
                ♣ A J 10 8 5 2

WEST	NORTH	EAST	SOUTH
	Pass(!)	Pass	Pass
1♠	Dbl	3♠	4♣
4♠	5♣	Pass	Pass
Dbl	All Pass		

This time, the bidding suggests that the high-card strength is more evenly divided. Even though North and South are passed hands, North may be bidding 5♣ to make. Moreover, if North-South have a big club fit, a trump lead may accomplish nothing.

West should be worried about getting a plus score. His best chance is to lead the ♥A, or perhaps the ♥Q, and continue hearts, hoping to establish a winner. If West leads a trump (or the ♦K or a spade), he'll regret it since declarer can establish the diamonds for two heart discards and make his doubled contract.

(Incidentally, I gave North's original pass an exclamation mark only because I fear almost everybody would open. Since North has borderline high-card values, no spade length and a ragged long suit, I agree with his pass.)

```
Dlr: South          ♠ K 8 3
Vul: N-S            ♥ A K 7 4
                    ♦ K 7
                    ♣ Q J 6 3
       ♠ 9 7 5 4                    ♠ Q J 10 6 2
       ♥ J                          ♥ 9
       ♦ A J 10 6 4                 ♦ Q 9 3
       ♣ A K 8                      ♣ 10 9 4 2
                    ♠ A
                    ♥ Q 10 8 6 5 3 2
                    ♦ 8 5 2
                    ♣ 7 5
```

WEST	NORTH	EAST	SOUTH
			2♥
Dbl	4♥	4♠	Pass
Pass	5♥	Pass	Pass
Dbl	All Pass		

I watched this deal in a competent IMP game. Against 5♥ doubled, West led a learned trump—a spectacular disaster. South deposited one of his club losers on the ♠K, led toward the ♦K and lost one diamond and one club.

Here, West couldn't be sure that it wasn't *East* who had sacrificed, so a trump lead was uncalled for. West should have led a pedestrian ♣K.

In the post-mortem, East tried to make his partner feel better by observing that even if West led a high club, he might switch to a spade at the second trick. (East couldn't signal count at the first trick since he might have held a doubleton club.) But I think not. South had to have something for his vulnerable weak two-bid: what other card could he have aside from the ♠A?

Slammed by Preemption

Good players often "bash" into games—especially vulnerable games—but slam bidding is usually a process of slow and careful investigation. If you go down in a speculative slam, you toss away a valuable game bonus.

Given a free run, most practiced partnerships are reasonably accurate in slam auctions. Without interference, some systems, such as "relay" methods, can be frighteningly precise. Nowadays, though, opponents make a nuisance of themselves by climbing into the auction with few values visible to the naked eye, disrupting the flow of information.

Try these problems, which occurred in expert IMP games:

1.
WEST	NORTH	EAST	SOUTH
3♥	Pass	4♥	?

Both sides vulnerable. What should South call with

♠ A Q 10 6 4   ♥ None   ♦ 5 2   ♣ A K 9 8 7 6   ?

2.
WEST	NORTH	EAST	SOUTH
1♣	1♦	3♣ (1)	?

(1) preemptive

E-W vulnerable. What should South call with

♠ A K Q 9 7 5   ♥ J 2   ♦ K J 3 2   ♣ J   ?

3.
WEST	NORTH	EAST	SOUTH
			1♥
Pass	2♦	4♠	?

North-South vulnerable. What should South call with

♠ A 10   ♥ K Q J 7 5 3   ♦ J   ♣ A K 6 5   ?

If South passes, North doubles. What should South do then?

4.
WEST	NORTH	EAST	SOUTH
			1♣
Pass	1♠	Pass	3♣
Pass	3NT	Pass	?

North-South vulnerable. South holds

♠ K Q J   ♥ J   ♦ 10 5 2   ♣ A K Q 9 6 2.

Do you agree with South 3♣ rebid? What call should he make now?

5.
WEST	NORTH	EAST	SOUTH
		3♥	Pass
4♥	4♠	Pass	?

Both sides vulnerable. What should South call with

♠ 9 8 7 2   ♥ A 10   ♦ A Q 10 9 7 6   ♣ 2   ?

As you may have guessed, problems 1 and 5 arose from the same deal.

```
Dlr: West          ♠ 9 8 7 2
Vul: Both          ♥ A 10
                   ♦ A Q 10 9 7 6
                   ♣ 2
      ♠ K                        ♠ J 5 3
      ♥ K Q J 8 7 6 3            ♥ 9 5 4 2
      ♦ J 3                      ♦ K 8 4
      ♣ J 5 3                    ♣ Q 10 4
                   ♠ A Q 10 6 4
                   ♥ —
                   ♦ 5 2
                   ♣ A K 9 8 7 6
```

WEST	NORTH	EAST	SOUTH
3♥	4♦(!)	4♥	4♠
All Pass			

Since North had four-card spade support and good controls, it seems he might have at least tried for slam. Perhaps he felt guilty because he didn't have his 4♦ bid. At 4♠ South contrived to lose two trump tricks, but if he had been at 6♠ he might have produced a successful safety play by cashing the ♠A early.

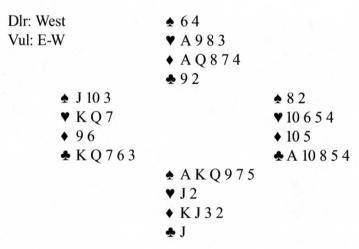

```
Dlr: West          ♠ 6 4
Vul: E-W           ♥ A 9 8 3
                   ♦ A Q 8 7 4
                   ♣ 9 2
      ♠ J 10 3                   ♠ 8 2
      ♥ K Q 7                    ♥ 10 6 5 4
      ♦ 9 6                      ♦ 10 5
      ♣ K Q 7 6 3                ♣ A 10 8 5 4
                   ♠ A K Q 9 7 5
                   ♥ J 2
                   ♦ K J 3 2
                   ♣ J
```

WEST	NORTH	EAST	SOUTH
1♣	1♦	3♣	4♠
All Pass			

The best slam was 6♦, but South also took 12 tricks at spades. North-South were fixed to some degree by West's featherweight opening bid and East's preemptive raise at unfavorable vulnerability. Nevertheless, South's jump to 4♠ looks like a rubber-bridge player's time-saving bid. To cue-bid 4♣ would have cost him nothing.

```
Dlr: South          ♠ 9 6
Vul: N-S            ♥ A 9
                    ♦ A Q 10 7 4 3
                    ♣ Q 7 3
    ♠ 7 3                           ♠ K Q J 8 5 4 2
    ♥ 8 6 4 2                       ♥ 10
    ♦ 9 6 5                         ♦ K 8 2
    ♣ J 10 9 4                      ♣ 8 2
                    ♠ A 10
                    ♥ K Q J 7 5 3
                    ♦ J
                    ♣ A K 6 5
```

WEST	NORTH	EAST	SOUTH
			1♥
Pass	2♦	4♠	Pass
Pass	Dbl	Pass	5♣
All Pass			

East's preempt left North-South to grope, but South's bidding hardly portrayed a hand with such massive slam potential. South did manage to make 5♣, but 4♠ doubled would have cost 800, and South would have taken 13 tricks at hearts after a spade opening lead with a winning ruffing finesse in diamonds.

What do these deals teach? Conventional wisdom states that when your partner acts over a preempt, you should give him plenty of room. One authority suggested discounting your first six high-card points Nevertheless, you can lose by being too conservative as well as by being too bold. Don't mastermind; don't make a final decision when you can't know it's right. If you think you may have a slam, make a try. Don't neglect to bid the value of the cards.

Opposing preemption isn't always damaging. Look at this deal.

```
Dlr: South          ♠ A 10 8 6 4
Vul: N-S            ♥ Q 9 4
IMPs                ♦ A 7 3
                    ♣ J 3
      ♠ 7 3                        ♠ 9 5 2
      ♥ A 8 6 5 2                  ♥ K 10 7 3
      ♦ K 9 4                      ♦ Q J 8 4
      ♣ 8 7 4                      ♣ 10 5
                    ♠ K Q J
                    ♥ J
                    ♦ 10 5 2
                    ♣ A K Q 9 6 2
```

WEST	NORTH	EAST	SOUTH
			1♣
Pass	1♠	Pass	3♣
Pass	3NT	All Pass	

South was reluctant to pass 3NT, but for all he knew, North had a hand such as 10654,KQ3,AJ4,765. Perhaps South should have supported the spades at his second turn.

At one table, East-West indulged in some fatuous interference that backfired:

WEST	NORTH	EAST	SOUTH
			1♣
1♥(!)	1♠ (1)	2♥	3♠
Pass	4♦	Pass	4NT
Pass	5♥	Pass	6♠
All Pass			

(1) no negative double, hence a five-card or longer suit

Thanks to the busy East-West bidding, North-South not only knew to avoid notrump and play at their spade fit, North was encouraged to make a slam try that South accepted. Plus 1430!

At My Club

Dlr: South		♠ J 7 6 5 3 2	
Vul: Both		♥ 4	
		♦ J 6	
		♣ Q 8 5 3	

♠ 9	♠ Q 10 8 4
♥ 10 9 7 6 2	♥ 8
♦ K Q 10 7 4	♦ 9 8 5 3 2
♣ A 6	♣ K 7 2

♠ A K
♥ A K Q J 5 3
♦ A
♣ J 10 9 4

WEST	NORTH	EAST	SOUTH
			2♣
Pass	2♦	Pass	2♥
Pass	2♠	Pass	4♥
All Pass			

Opening lead: ♦K

My friend the English professor made one of his infrequent appearances at the club a couple of days ago. The prof has a low tolerance level for both bad play and improper use of the English language. He chastised me once for writing that a contract "foundered and sank."

"It's a redundancy," the prof advised me. "'Founder' has a built-in sink. That's what the word means."

I was sitting in the club lounge with the professor when a member came over and asked him if "abstemiously" is the only English word that has all six vowels in order.

"Abstemiously," mused the prof. "It means 'not in excess.'"

"The word usually refers to eating and drinking in moderation, doesn't it?" I asked.

"True," the prof replied, "but some of my partners would do well to be abstemious about drawing trumps."

That afternoon the prof sat in for a few deals of rubber bridge, and I watched a deal in which he had to suffer as dummy. South, playing at 4♥, took the ♦A and promptly began to draw trumps. When he cashed the A-K, however, East discarded a spade, and South found himself in hot water. He took the Q-J of trumps and led the ♣J, and East won and led another diamond. South ruffed, took his ♠AK and led another club, but West produced the ace and cashed the ♥10, drawing South's last trump. West then took two diamonds for down two.

"What luck," South sighed.

The prof groaned. "If you weren't such a glutton for drawing trumps, you'd make the contract. You have only two top losers, so you can afford to lose a club ruff. Lead the ♣J at the second trick. If the defense takes the ace and king, ruffs the next club, and forces you to ruff a diamond, you can draw trumps—even if they broke 5-1—and take the rest.

"If instead they win the first club and force you to ruff a diamond," the prof went on, "you lead another club. If they lead a third diamond, you can ruff in dummy, keeping control, and you're safe."

"Is 'abstemiously' really the only word with a, e, i, o, u and y in order?" I asked the prof.

"Maybe," he said facetiously.

PART the FIFTH

Sit Beside Me

Late in a one-session Sectional pair game, I estimate us at a couple of boards above average – enough to place but not nearly enough to win. Only the opponents are vulnerable, and I'm South, the dealer, with

♠ A J 8
♥ 10 6
♦ A Q 9 4 2
♣ K 8 3

I believe in discipline above all else, but if I'm ever going to take a flyer, it's now. We are playing Standard methods, but I open a "strong" 1NT. I'm supposed to have at least 15 good points, but my hand is almost worth that, and the vulnerability is favorable. Maybe I can steal the contract for -50 or -100 when the opponents can take eight or nine tricks at a major.

Nothing of the sort happens. The opponents aren't interested, and my partner raises to 3NT, passed out. I hope he has either a little extra strength or a sense of humor.

West leads the ♠K, and when dummy hits, I see my efforts to avoid a normal contract have been wasted.

♠ 7 5 3
♥ A J 4
♦ J 8 6 5 3
♣ A J

♠ A J 8
♥ 10 6
♦ A Q 9 4 2
♣ K 8 3

WEST	NORTH	EAST	SOUTH
			1NT(!)
Pass	3NT	All Pass	

East follows with the ♠4, and I play low. I don't expect West to continue spades into my A-J, but I'd rather have him lead to the second trick.

West thinks for a half a minute and shifts to the ♥Q. I don't mind that. Nine tricks are safe now, but no doubt I'll need an overtrick or two for a good matchpoint result. I take dummy's ♥A — East plays the nine — and lead the ♦J. I intend to finesse — the percentage play with this combination — and leading the jack gains if East has K-10-7.

My finesse loses, and West leads another heart. East wins with the king and returns a spade, and I take the ace and cash the ♦A. West follows with the ten, and East throws a heart.

I have nine tricks: four diamonds, two hearts, a spade and two clubs. Should I lead a club to the jack for an overtrick? If East has the ♣Q and has a spade left, I'll go down, but I think the finesse is a big favorite. West started with two diamonds and presumably two hearts, and if he had only four spades, he'd have five clubs and might have led a club. A stronger indication is that if West had worthless clubs, he'd probably have led a club at the second trick instead of the ♥Q. For all West knew, my hearts could have been K-10-x.

When I try the club finesse, it wins, and I take ten tricks for +430. The full deal:

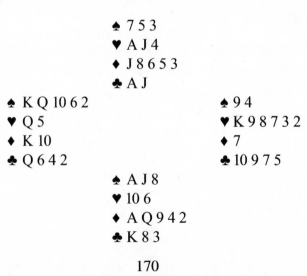

```
                 ♠ 7 5 3
                 ♥ A J 4
                 ♦ J 8 6 5 3
                 ♣ A J
    ♠ K Q 10 6 2              ♠ 9 4
    ♥ Q 5                     ♥ K 9 8 7 3 2
    ♦ K 10                    ♦ 7
    ♣ Q 6 4 2                 ♣ 10 9 7 5
                 ♠ A J 8
                 ♥ 10 6
                 ♦ A Q 9 4 2
                 ♣ K 8 3
```

170

"You had only 14 points," my partner says accusingly.

Almost every North-South reached 3NT. When South opened 1♦, West overcalled 1♠. North usually cue-bid 2♠, suggesting a diamond limit raise or better, and South converted to 3NT. Still, our +430 scored above average since some Wests shifted to a club at the second trick. The defenders discarded carefully, and South got no second heart trick and took only nine tricks in all.

At my table, West would have held me to nine tricks by shifting to a club or a low heart at the second trick. In fact, if he leads a low heart, I must guess to put up dummy's ace to make even 3NT.

In the first match after the break in a Sectional Swiss Teams, only the opponents are vulnerable, and as East I hold

♠ A J 9 2
♥ 9 6 3
♦ A 8 2
♣ K 9 3

North, the dealer, opens 1♥. Ordinarily, I wouldn't think of climbing into the auction with a hand better for defense, but my partner for the day is as conservative as they come and I've been trying to compensate. Suppose I pass, South raises to 2♥ and there are two passes. Then I can balance with a double, but my partner won't play me for this much strength and may misjudge and let the opponents play 3♥ when we can make 3♠.

So I step out of character with a double. At least I have no wasted honors in hearts. Some players might try a 1♠ overcall, but I'm enough of a curmudgeon to believe that an overcall promises a five-card suit and should deliver one. If I overcall, West is equally likely to misjudge in a competitive auction.

South redoubles. I may have gotten us into the soup. My partner bids 2♣ and North rebids 2♥. As most pairs play, North should have a weakish, distributional hand with no desire to double us. I pass thankfully, and South jumps to 3NT. Everyone passes, West leads the ♣5 and dummy is as I expect.

♠ Q 10 5
♥ A K Q 10 7 5
♦ 10 3
♣ 10 4

♠ A J 9 2
♥ 9 6 3
♦ A 8 2
♣ K 9 3

WEST	NORTH	EAST	SOUTH
	1♥	Dbl	Redbl
2♣	2♥	Pass	3NT
All Pass			

Dummy plays the ♣10, and I put my king on the table—face down to give myself a moment to think about the entire defense. When I face my card, South takes the ace. He leads a heart to dummy and returns the ♦10.

I know South has six heart tricks, and I suspect he has the ♣AQ. If he had only the ace, he'd have held up; if A-J-x, he'd have played low from dummy on the first club to assure a second stopper.

Even if South has the ♦KJ, he won't mis-guess if I play low. He'll place me with the ace for my double and put up the king for his ninth trick. What if South has the ♦QJ? Then I can grab the ♦A and continue clubs, setting up West's clubs while he has the ♦K as an entry. But that's no good. South's leap to 3NT suggests opening values, and if had a hand such as

♠ K 7 4 3 ♥ J 4 ♦ Q J 9 4 ♣ A Q 6,

he'd have led a spade at the second trick to set up his ninth trick.

We seem to have only one chance, so I take the ♦A and shift to a low spade. Fortunately, the full deal is:

```
                    ♠ Q 10 5
                    ♥ A K Q 10 7 5
                    ♦ 10 3
                    ♣ 10 4
    ♠ K 6                           ♠ A J 9 2
    ♥ 8 2                           ♥ 9 6 3
    ♦ J 7 6 5                       ♦ A 8 2
    ♣ J 8 7 5 2                     ♣ K 9 3
                    ♠ 8 7 4 3
                    ♥ J 4
                    ♦ K Q 9 4
                    ♣ A Q 6
```

West produces the king and returns a spade, and I score three more spades for down one.

Alas, we didn't gain on the deal. At the other table our teammates reached 4♥, and East led a trump. North drew trumps and led a diamond, but when East took the ace, he could count ten tricks for declarer: six hearts, two clubs with a finesse and two diamonds. So East shifted to a low spade as *his* only chance.

Early in a match in a local Knockout Teams, both sides are vulnerable, and as South I hold

```
                    ♠ J 3
                    ♥ K J 6
                    ♦ A Q 4
                    ♣ 10 8 6 4 2
```

My partner deals and opens 1♠, and East overcalls 2♥.

I have 11 points — ordinarily enough values to invite game — but I judge this hand worth more. East's two-level overcall has increased the positional value of my heart honors. If East has the ♥AQ, my K-J-6 is worth as much as A-K-6. Since we're vulnerable and have more to gain than to lose by bidding game, I think I'll spare my partner a guess and bid 3NT. I'd stretch to invite game if my ♦A were the ♦K.

I do have one option. I could pass and pass again if North reopened with a double. That looks hungry to me. If I were sure we could beat 2♥ doubled two for +500, I might try for a penalty since the odds would be favorable. We'd lose at most 3 IMPs and would gain 12 if a game failed in the replay. But if East has a little extra distribution, he'd go down only one and might even make 2♥, and then I'd have to explain being -670 to my teammates.

When I jump to 3NT, everyone passes. West leads the ♥10, and dummy hits with moderate values.

```
              ♠ A K 10 8 4
              ♥ 7 3
              ♦ K 9 6
              ♣ Q J 7

              ♠ J 3
              ♥ K J 6
              ♦ A Q 4
              ♣ 10 8 6 4 2
```

WEST	NORTH	EAST	SOUTH
	1♠	2♥	3NT
All Pass			

East puts up the ♥A and returns the ♥5. I play my jack, winning. So far, so good.

I have two heart tricks and three diamonds, so four spades will be enough. At the second trick I lead the ♣J, intending to let it ride and hoping I don't lose to a dry queen. Instead, West covers with the queen, dummy wins and East follows with the six.

At matchpoint scoring, I'd have to consider the possibility of an overtrick (although on the bidding, a 3-3 spade break is unlikely). At IMPs I can and should play safe. I come back to my ♦A and lead another spade, and when West plays low, I ask for dummy's eight. If East can win, spades have split no worse than 4-2, and the rest of dummy's spades will score.

But, sure enough, East discards. That doesn't surprise me since he rated to have a shapely hand to overcall vulnerable at the two level. I save time by claiming nine tricks. The full deal:

```
              ♠ A K 10 8 4
              ♥ 7 3
              ♦ K 9 6
              ♣ Q J 7
♠ Q 9 7 5 2                      ♠ 6
♥ 10 9 4                         ♥ A Q 8 5 2
♦ J 7 3                          ♦ 10 8 5 2
♣ 9 5                            ♣ A K 3
              ♠ J 3
              ♥ K J 6
              ♦ A Q 4
              ♣ 10 8 6 4 2
```

The board was worth a 9-IMP gain to us. At the other table, the auction started the same way, but South chose the pass that didn't appeal to me. North duly reopened with a double, passed out, and South led the ♣J: queen, king, six. North could have achieved down two with a trump shift, but he tried to cash the ♠A. East ruffed, took the top clubs, ruffed his low club in dummy and led a diamond. The defense couldn't stop him from winning his fourth diamond or ruffing it in dummy, so the contract was down only one, +200 to North-South.

In a Sectional Open Pairs, both sides are vulnerable, and as South I hold

```
♠ 4 2
♥ 6 5
♦ A Q J 10 9 5 4
♣ A 7
```

East, the dealer, passes, and I open 1♦. With two and a half defensive tricks and 2-2-7-2 distribution, this is not a hand to preempt, particularly after one opponent has already passed. West passes, my partner responds 1♥ and East comes in with a double.

I was about to rebid 2♦, but now I can describe my hand with a jump to 3♦. If I had 17 or so points with six good diamonds, I'd redouble. If I had less strength I could pass or rebid 2♦. But a jump to 3♦ over the double has a preemptive flavor. I'm suggesting long diamonds but minimum values.

175

I fail to shut out West. He leaps to 5♣. North tries 5♦, and everyone passes. West leads the ♠9, and dummy's values are not quite what I need.

♠ K 10 5 3
♥ A Q 3 2
♦ K 8 7 6
♣ 5

♠ 4 2
♥ 6 5
♦ A Q J 10 9 5 4
♣ A 7

WEST	NORTH	EAST	SOUTH
		Pass	1♦
Pass	1♥	Dbl	3♦
5♣	5♦	All Pass	

If North had the ♥K instead of the ♠K, 5♦ would be a laydown. As it is, the ♠K looks worthless, and I may have three losers.

I cover with the ♠10, and East wins with the jack and shifts to the ♣2. I take the ace, and West follows with the king. If West started with the ♣KQ or ♣KQJ, East must have the ♥K for his double.

I can try for a throw-in. If I draw trumps, ruff my low club and lead a low spade from dummy, East will be end played if he wins. But he should be able to tell that I have two spades and two hearts: if I had three spades, I wouldn't lead a second spade. If East correctly played low, West would win and shift to a heart, and I'd have no chance.

Fortunately, I don't have to play for a defensive error. I can get home if I guess East's distribution. I ruff my low club in dummy and cash all seven of my trumps. East shows up with a singleton trump, and his lead of the ♣2 suggested four. I'm sure his distribution was 4-4-1-4. With three tricks left, the position is

176

```
            ♠ K
            ♥ A Q
            ♦
            ♣


            ♠ 4
            ♥ 6 5
            ♦
            ♣
```

East has discarded some clubs, two hearts, the ♠6 and the ♠Q. Trusting my view of East's shape, I exit with a spade, and East wins and must lead from his ♥K to dummy's A-Q. The full deal:

```
                    ♠ K 10 5 3
                    ♥ A Q 3 2
                    ♦ K 8 7 6
                    ♣ 5
    ♠ 9 8 7                            ♠ A Q J 6
    ♥ J 9 7                            ♥ K 10 8 4
    ♦ 3                                ♦ 2
    ♣ K Q J 9 4 3                      ♣ 10 8 6 2
                    ♠ 4 2
                    ♥ 6 5
                    ♦ A Q J 10 9 5 4
                    ♣ A 7
```

If East had bared his ♥K to save two spades, I'd have led a heart to the ace.

At the other table, South opened 1♦, but West jumped to 3♣ despite the vulnerability. North made a negative double, East raised to 4♣, and after two passes, North tried 5♦. West led the ♣K, and South gave the hand a straightforward play. He drew trumps and finessed in hearts and then in spades to go down one.

East's double at my table was a losing action. If he had passed, I doubt I'd have made 5♦. Players often enter the auction without assessing the chance that their side will declare. If the opponents are likely to buy the deal, intervention will help them judge the play and maybe the bidding as well.

As I See It

The Current Epidemic

IMPs, neither side vulnerable. You hold

♠ Q 3
♥ K 10
♦ A K J 8 7 2
♣ A 4 3

There are three passes to you. What is your call?

I admit to being a hypochondriac—my wife says that if I visited the Dead Sea, I'd try to find out what it died of—and I am all too keenly aware of unpleasant bugs. I am even more aware that unsound bidding practices tend to spread like an epidemic.

The deal below, from a U.S. Trials, made an impression on me more than 30 years ago. All the players were top experts.

Dlr: North	♠ —	
Vul: E-W	♥ A K 8 6 5	
	♦ 10 8 6 2	
	♣ J 10 7 3	

♠ A K J 6 4 2		♠ 10 9 8 7 5
♥ 7		♥ J 10 9 4
♦ Q J		♦ 3
♣ K Q 8 6		♣ 5 4 2

	♠ Q 3	
	♥ Q 3 2	
	♦ A K 9 7 5 4	
	♣ A 9	

Table 1

WEST	NORTH	EAST	SOUTH
	Pass	Pass	1NT(!)
Dbl (1)	Redbl	2♣	2♦
2♠	3♠	Dbl	Pass
Pass	Redbl	Pass	3NT
Pass	4♦	Pass	5♦
All Pass			

(1) unspecified one-suiter

Table 2

WEST	NORTH	EAST	SOUTH
	Pass	Pass	1NT(!)
2♠	Dbl (1)	Pass	3♦
Pass	3♥	3♠	4♥
4♠	5♥	Pass	Pass
5♠	All Pass(!)		

(1) takeout

North-South at table 1 played their excellent grand slam at a game but gained IMPs when North-South at table 2 sold out to 5♠ undoubled for +100.

Edgar Kaplan attributed both results to South's 1NT opening. "The off-shape 1NT strikes again," Kaplan wrote tartly. I agree, though it seems that South at table 1 could have gone to 6♦ if he had trusted North's bidding at all.

This deal turned me against opening 1NT with a flawed pattern. In the past three decades, I have seen nothing to suggest that players gain by distorting notrump openings; but from what I've seen and heard lately, goofy 1NT openings have reached a stage where we need the Centers for Disease Control to intervene. Such openings are another symptom of the trend in which players indulge in actions that trivialize the partnership nature of the game.

On the net:

```
Dlr: North              ♠ A J 8 5
Vul: None               ♥ 6 5 4
IMPs                    ♦ Q 9 4
                        ♣ K 6 5
        ♠ Q 3                       ♠ 9 4 2
        ♥ K 10                      ♥ A J 8 2
        ♦ A K J 8 7 2               ♦ 10 5 3
        ♣ A 4 3                     ♣ Q J 9
                        ♠ K 10 7 6
                        ♥ Q 9 7 3
                        ♦ 6
                        ♣ 10 8 7 2
```

WEST	NORTH	EAST	SOUTH
	Pass	Pass	Pass
1NT(!)	Pass	2♣	Pass
2♦	Pass	2NT	Pass
3NT	All Pass		

3NT was a poor spot. Even if the defenders didn't run the spades on the go, they would get another chance if declarer lost a trick to the ♦Q.

The deal was played more than 50 times, and at almost every table West had to choose an opening bid in fourth position. I regret to report that 22 Wests caught a bug and tried 1NT—a misbid as well as a significant underbid. A slim plurality of 24 Wests opened 1♦.

After a 1NT opening, some Easts passed, and West scored +120. Other Easts raised, and West played at 3NT and almost invariably went down.

Many pairs went minus even when West opened 1♦ and East responded 1♥. Some Wests jumped to 2NT next and went down at 3NT. If West rebid 3♦, some Easts closed their eyes and tried 3NT, down again. A couple of Easts bid 3♠(!) next, and whatever they had in mind, it didn't work: their side bit the dust at 3NT or 4♥.

One East raised West's 3♦ rebid to 4♦, a questionable action when he had so many losers. I believe most experts would treat 4♦ as forcing (though I wouldn't), and West indeed went on to 5♦, down.

At another table the auction began this way:

WEST	NORTH	EAST	SOUTH
	Pass	Pass	Pass
1♦	1♠(!)	Pass	3♠

"See," a 1NT opener might say. "Unless I give a picture of my strength and pattern at my first turn, competition may freeze me out."

"A player disciplined enough to open 1♦," I reply, "will be disciplined enough to pass 3♠, which will go down at least one, giving East-West a plus." West actually bid 4♦ and went minus even though East judged well to pass.

At only five tables did East-West have a sane and sober auction: 1♦-1♥, 3♦-Pass. Making three, +110.

What happened to 3NT at the table I watched? North led the ♥6, and West won with the ten, cashed the top diamonds and led a third diamond. Alas, South discarded the ♣8 and ♣2. Whether he was misguidedly signaling "count" or thought he was playing "upside-down attitude," the effect was fatal. North shifted to the ♣5, playing South for the ♣A and ♠Q, and declarer triumphed in with an overtrick.

No doubt West will open 1NT on that hand again. Players who take flyers remember their good results and dismiss their bad results as "unlucky."

Blame Game

When I played in local team events, we'd have fun with late-night "charge sessions" at the neighborhood tavern. Every adjudged error cost the perpetrator a quarter, and the money went into a pot that paid for the beer and pizza.

Many players aren't as convivial about mistakes. We all know players who think it's not whether you win or lose but how you place the blame. They're more interested in winning the post-mortem than the event. Moreover, "Whose fault?" and "Apportion the blame" pleas turn up everywhere from magazines to on-line message boards.

Here are two deals I watched on the net. You apportion the blame.

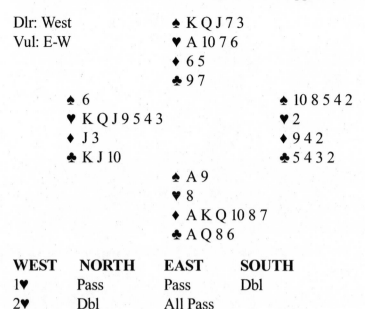

Dlr: West
Vul: E-W

```
                    ♠ K Q J 7 3
                    ♥ A 10 7 6
                    ♦ 6 5
                    ♣ 9 7
    ♠ 6                             ♠ 10 8 5 4 2
    ♥ K Q J 9 5 4 3                 ♥ 2
    ♦ J 3                           ♦ 9 4 2
    ♣ K J 10                        ♣ 5 4 3 2
                    ♠ A 9
                    ♥ 8
                    ♦ A K Q 10 8 7
                    ♣ A Q 8 6
```

WEST	NORTH	EAST	SOUTH
1♥	Pass	Pass	Dbl
2♥	Dbl	All Pass	

North-South were +500 against 2♥ doubled but could make 7♦ for +1440. (After the lead of the ♥K, South runs the trumps and then four spades, squeezing West in hearts and clubs. South must guess that spades are 5-1 and pitch a spade from dummy—a taxing play but not impossible given West's vulnerable bidding.)

North's pass over 1♥ was odd, of course, but not fatal. South's final pass was questionable, but he had a fine defensive hand and no doubt expected West to go for his life. I like North's double least: to "headhunt" for a penalty when you have unexplored offensive possibilities is wrong, and North had first-round heart control and winners in spades. Moreover, West could see the vulnerability when he bid 2♥. His pattern was hardly likely to be 2-5-3-3.

How about one of these sequences?

WEST	NORTH	EAST	SOUTH
1♥	1♠	Pass	2♥
Pass	2♠	Pass	4♦
Pass	4♥	Pass	5♣
Pass	5♦	Pass	5♠
Pass	7♦	All Pass	

or

WEST	NORTH	EAST	SOUTH
1♥	Pass	Pass	Dbl
2♥	3♠	Pass	4♦
Pass	4♠	Pass	5♣
Pass	5♥	Pass	7♦

Yes, they're fanciful. In real life I wouldn't expect many pairs to reach 7♦ or make it. But even 6♦ or 6♠ would outscore +500.

Dlr: North
Vul: N-S

```
                ♠ 9 8
                ♥ A K Q 10
                ♦ K 9 8 3
                ♣ A Q 8
  ♠ A 2                        ♠ K 10 6 5 4 3
  ♥ 7 4                        ♥ 5 3
  ♦ A 7 5 4                    ♦ Q 10 6 2
  ♣ J 6 5 4 3                  ♣ 7
                ♠ Q J 7
                ♥ J 9 8 6 2
                ♦ J
                ♣ K 10 9 2
```

WEST	NORTH	EAST	SOUTH
	1♦	2♠	Pass
Pass	Dbl	Pass	3♥
All Pass			

South took 11 tricks—West, trying to beat 3♥, ate his ♦A—but 4♥ was unbeatable.

If you asked two experts, you might get conflicting views:

"South should have jumped to 4♥ over the double." Perhaps, but North would have reopened with fewer values, and game would be an underdog even if he held a sound hand such as

```
                ♠ 9 8
                ♥ A 7 5 3
                ♦ A K 7 6 2
                ♣ A 6
```

"North should have raised 3♥ to 4♥."

Perhaps, but South had promised nothing aside from 13 cards. What if he'd had

> ♠ Q 6 5 2
> ♥ J 8 6 4
> ♦ 7 6 5
> ♣ J 6   ?

If you put goat's horns on either North or South, I understand, but not every bad result is culpable. If I were assessing blame on this deal, I'd give it to the player clearly responsible for the disaster: East, who picked the right time for a good obstructive move.

Slam Questions

Here are three bidding problems taken from IMP games on the net.

(1) As South, you hold

> ♠ Q 10 4
> ♥ Q 8 4 2
> ♦ Q 3
> ♣ A J 9 4

WEST	NORTH	EAST	SOUTH
			Pass
Pass	1♦	Pass	1♥
Pass	2♠	Pass	3♣
Pass	4♥	Pass	5♣
Pass	5♦	Pass	?

Do you agree with your bidding? What do say now?

(2) You hold

> ♠ Q 7 5 3
> ♥ A 10 9 7 6 4
> ♦ K Q 5
> ♣ —

As the dealer, you open 1♥, and your partner responds 1♠. What call do you make?

(3) This time you're West with

♠ A 8 7 6
♥ 9 2
♦ A K J
♣ A K 6 3

WEST	NORTH	EAST	SOUTH
	Pass	Pass	Pass
1♣	2♦	2♥	Pass
2♠	Pass	4♠	Pass
?			

What call do you make? What call would you make if East had raised to 3♠? Do you agree with your 2♠ bid?

These three slam deals all appeared within the space of an hour in an expert game. I thought each contained the germ of a bidding principle.

(1) Dlr: South
     Vul: E-W

```
                 ♠ A K J 5
                 ♥ A K 9
                 ♦ A J 10 5 4
                 ♣ 6
   ♠ 7 6                        ♠ 9 8 3 2
   ♥ J 10 7 3                   ♥ 6 5
   ♦ 8 7 6                      ♦ K 9 2
   ♣ K Q 8 2                    ♣ 10 7 5 3
                 ♠ Q 10 4
                 ♥ Q 8 4 2
                 ♦ Q 3
                 ♣ A J 9 4
```

WEST	NORTH	EAST	SOUTH
			Pass
Pass	1♦	Pass	1♥
Pass	2♠	Pass	3♣
Pass	4♥	Pass	5♣
Pass	5♦	Pass	5♥
Pass	5♠	Pass	6♥
All Pass			

186

West led the ♣K, and although 6♥ wasn't a hopeless slam, it went down. The best slam, especially at IMPs, and the only makable slam against best defense was 6♦, but diamonds barely got a mention as a possible trump suit.

The trouble started when South bid 3♣, suggesting a more distributional hand, instead of bidding 2NT or 3NT. North's leap to 4♥ was understandable. He thought South had at least five hearts and wanted to show strong three-card support, reassuring South about trump quality.

South compounded his error when he failed to try 6♦ at either of his last two turns. North's bidding had implied long diamonds, and South's Q-x was significant support. Since every honor South held except the ♣J was working, South could have committed to slam opposite the powerful hand North had shown.

Principles: make the bid that best describes your hand; support your partner.

(2) Dlr: North
     Vul: None

    ♠ Q 7 5 3
    ♥ A 10 9 7 6 4
    ♦ K Q 5
    ♣

    ♠ A K J 6
    ♥ J 2
    ♦ 8 6 4 2
    ♣ A Q 9

WEST	NORTH	EAST	SOUTH
	1♥	Pass	1♠
Pass	4♣	Dbl	Redbl
Pass	4♠	Pass	6♠
All Pass			

This slam had no play even after a club opening lead. Some players might blame South for his leap to 6♠, but I can't. If I had 15 good-looking points opposite a partner who had tried for slam after my 1♠ response, I might have bid slam also.

Splinter bids are valuable tools, but bidding accuracy suffers when players use them with a wide range of hands. North made a common mistake, in my view: he overbid his high-card values. To invite a slam with that North hand wouldn't have occurred to me. I'd have settled for a conservative raise to 2♠, expecting more bidding.

Principle: a splinter bid at the level of game invites slam; if you don't have slam values, don't splinter.

(3) Dlr: North
Vul: Both

```
                    ♠ J 3 2
                    ♥ 10
                    ♦ Q 10 9 7 4 3
                    ♣ Q 9 4
    ♠ A 8 7 6                      ♠ K Q 10 4
    ♥ 9 2                          ♥ K Q 8 4 3
    ♦ A K J                        ♦ 8 6
    ♣ A K 6 3                      ♣ 8 7
                    ♠ 9 5
                    ♥ A J 7 6 5
                    ♦ 5 2
                    ♣ J 10 5 2
```

WEST	NORTH	EAST	SOUTH
	Pass	Pass	Pass
1♣	2♦	2♥	Pass
2♠	Pass	4♠	Pass
6♠	All Pass		

If East had been a believer in the "principle of fast arrival," he might have raised to only 3♠, leaving more room for a slam hunt. In that style, a raise to 4♠ would have suggested stopping at game. Personally, I believe 4♠ shouldn't deny slam interest but should show a decent hand and emphasize strong trumps.

6♠ went down quickly. North led his singleton heart and got a ruff. Perhaps West's leap to slam was too bold. His ♦J looked worthless, East was a passed hand, and—most significant—North's vulnerable preempt warned of bad splits that might endanger a high-level contract.

At another table, West not only declined to try for slam, he declined to look for a spade fit. Over East's 2♥, West jumped to 3NT, passed out. He took nine tricks.

I'm not enough of a result merchant to recommend West's bid: 4♠ could have been East-West's correct contract. But the leap to 3NT was defensible and did in fact gain IMPs.

Principle: an opponent's preempt elevates the chance of bad breaks; with a close decision in a constructive auction, be conservative.

At My Club

Dlr: South
Vul: N-S

♠ 4 3
♥ 8 6 3
♦ K Q 8 4 2
♣ 7 3 2

♠ J 8 7
♥ A 7
♦ 10 9 7 6 5 3
♣ 10 8

♠ 9 6
♥ K Q 10 9 4 2
♦ J
♣ Q J 9 6

♠ A K Q 10 5 2
♥ J 5
♦ A
♣ A K 5 4

WEST	NORTH	EAST	SOUTH
			2♣
Pass	2♦	3♥	3♠
Pass	4♠	All Pass	

"I saw it and still don't believe it."

Ed, my club's best player, was telling me about a deal he'd encountered against the redoubtable Minnie Bottoms. Minnie is 82 and wears ancient bifocals that make her mix up kings and jacks, usually to her opponents' chagrin. Against Ed's 4♠, Minnie led the ♥A and a low heart, and East took the queen and led the king.

"I didn't like my chances," Ed said. "I could ruff with the ten, but West figured to have the jack. If she overruffed, I'd be down one even if the clubs broke 3-3.

"Finally, I came up with a line of play that looked good. I knew East had a shapely hand to preempt, but she had only six hearts. If she had one trump or three clubs, I had no chance, so I gave her 2-6-1-4 distribution.

"I ruffed the third heart with the king." Ed went on. "I'd cash the ♦A, ♣AK and A-Q of trumps and throw Minnie in, I hoped, with the jack of trumps. If she had no more clubs, she'd have to lead a diamond to dummy, and my club losers would go away."

Ed's picture of the deal was on target, and he was due to make the contract. Alas, Minnie's bifocals got him.

"When I ruffed with the king of trumps," Ed sighed, "Minnie 'overruffed' with the jack. She thought I'd ruffed with the jack, and she had the king. Now I couldn't endplay her, and I lost two clubs and went down."

"Your technique was almost perfect," I consoled Ed. "But against Minnie, ruff the third heart with the ace of trumps."

Sit Beside Me

In a Regional Stratified Pairs, we're opposed by a seeded pair of experts. North-South are vulnerable, and as East I hold

♠ A K J 10 5 2
♥ 3
♦ 6 3
♣ J 10 9 3

This would be a solid weak two-bid if I were the dealer, but I'm in fourth position. South opens 1♥, West passes and North raises to 2♥.

To bid 2♠ would be easy enough, but in our style overcalls suggest sound high-card values, and my partner would expect more than I have. (Many players would overcall here with borderline values, fearing that if they passed and South passed, West would be unable to balance without spades. So East would bid as a so-called "pre-balance." This style requires partnership trust and fine table presence.) Since I have good playing strength, I choose instead to take advantage of the vulnerability and jump to 3♠. If I'm doubled I shouldn't be hurt badly, and I'll take away South's ability to make a game try at the three level.

As it happens, my preempt avails nothing. South bids 4♥, and everyone passes. West leads the ♠8.

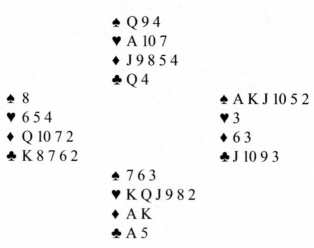

                    ♠ Q 9 4
                    ♥ A 10 7
                    ♦ J 9 8 5 4
                    ♣ Q 4
                                      ♠ A K J 10 5 2
                                      ♥ 3
                                      ♦ 6 3
                                      ♣ J 10 9 3

WEST	NORTH	EAST	SOUTH
			1♥
Pass	2♥	3♠	4♥
All Pass			

That's a fairly strong dummy, but its ♠Q is wasted. Maybe we have a chance for a set.

Our chances seem to improve when I take the ♠10 and cash the king, and West discards the ♣8. On my ♠A, he throws the ♣7. We have our book, and I shift to a club without giving it much thought.

South produces the ♣A. He cashes the ♦AK, leads the ♥K to dummy's ace, ruffs a diamond high, leads the ♥8 to the ten and ruffs a diamond high. South then produces the ♥2, and dummy wins with the seven and has a good diamond, on which South throws a club. He wins the 13th trick with a trump, making four. The full deal is:

                    ♠ Q 9 4
                    ♥ A 10 7
                    ♦ J 9 8 5 4
                    ♣ Q 4
    ♠ 8   ♠ A K J 10 5 2
    ♥ 6 5 4   ♥ 3
    ♦ Q 10 7 2   ♦ 6 3
    ♣ K 8 7 6 2   ♣ J 10 9 3
                    ♠ 7 6 3
                    ♥ K Q J 9 8 2
                    ♦ A K
                    ♣ A 5

"Sorry," I apologize. "If I shift to a trump at the fourth trick, I kill one of dummy's entries, and he can't score the long diamond. I relaxed when you signaled high in clubs."

"If I had the ♣A," my partner shrugs, "I'd ruff your good spade at the third trick and cash it."

He was right, but when I thought about the deal later, I was able to unload a little of my guilt. If my partner had held Q-x-x or J-x-x-x in trumps, he wouldn't have appreciated a trump shift. Only he knew that he had three low trumps and a double stopper in diamonds as well as the ♣K. He should have ruffed the third spade to lead a trump.

In a Regional Swiss Teams, my team's record stands at 5 and 1 when we meet one of the top teams entered. The first two boards are uneventful, and then as East I pick up

> ♠ 10 7
> ♥ K 10 2
> ♦ K 10 5 3
> ♣ 7 6 4 2

Neither side is vulnerable. My partner, the dealer, opens 1♦, and North passes.

Luckily, we aren't using inverted minor-suit raises; I'd be reluctant to even consider raising to 3♦. Since some response would be mandatory, I suppose I'd try 1NT. As it is, I can raise to 2♦. South then comes in with 2♠, West competes with 3♦ and North jumps to 4♠, passed out.

West leads the ♦4, and I see this dummy:

> ♠ 9 6 4 2
> ♥ J 8 6 3
> ♦ Q
> ♣ K Q J 5

> ```
>             ♠ 10 7
>         N   ♥ K 10 2
>     W  +  E ♦ K 10 5 3
>         S   ♣ 7 6 4 2
> ```

WEST	NORTH	EAST	SOUTH
1♦	Pass	2♦	2♠
3♦	4♠	All Pass	

North has taken a reasonable shot at game. South can have many hands that will make 4♠ cold or at least give it a chance.

I cover dummy's ♦Q with my king, and South takes the ace and considers. In due time he shakes his head and lays down the ♠A. My partner deposits the king, and South continues with the ♠Q, West pitching a diamond. South next leads a club. West grabs his ace and leads a low heart, but the full deal is

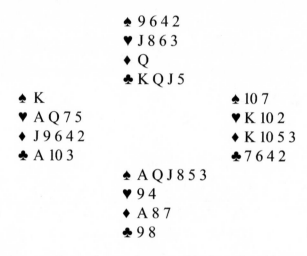

```
              ♠ 9 6 4 2
              ♥ J 8 6 3
              ♦ Q
              ♣ K Q J 5
♠ K                         ♠ 10 7
♥ A Q 7 5                   ♥ K 10 2
♦ J 9 6 4 2                 ♦ K 10 5 3
♣ A 10 3                    ♣ 7 6 4 2
              ♠ A Q J 8 5 3
              ♥ 9 4
              ♦ A 8 7
              ♣ 9 8
```

Since we can take only two hearts, South makes his game for +420. West and I look at each other and shrug.

At the other table, West opened 1♦ again. This time East-West were using inverted minors, and East experimented with a 1♥ response. South overcalled 1♠, and West raised to 2♥. I'd have been tempted to bid 4♠ as North since South would seem likely to have a singleton heart, but North settled for an invitational jump to 3♠. That wasn't enough encouragement for South.

Against 3♠ West led the ♥A and another heart, and South ruffed the third heart and wound up +140 when he lost a trump finesse to the bare king. We conceded 7 IMPs, a bad omen. Did we do anything to deserve a loss, do you think, or was it just a misfortune of war?

I missed a chance for a beautiful play. At the first trick, I should have played a low diamond! This couldn't cost—declarer could have no useful discard from dummy on his ♦A—but it might cause him to misplace the missing honors.

As the play went, South inferred that I had a high heart since West hadn't led one, and South had seen me play the ♦K. So South knew West held the ♠K for his opening bid. If I withhold my ♦K, South may place me with the ♠K and finesse to lose four tricks.

Regarding the bidding, most experts use "inverted minors." I don't care for them, partly because it's awkward to offer a weak jump raise on some hand types and partly because few partnerships—and certainly no casual partnerships—have firm agreements on what later bids mean. It won't do to sit down and say, "Let's play inverted minors," and let it go at that.

In a Regional Stratified Pairs, neither side is vulnerable, and I'm South, in third position, with

> ♠ A K 10 9 4 3
> ♥ A
> ♦ Q 10
> ♣ Q 9 8 3

After two passes, I open 1♠, and my partner responds 2NT. If he hadn't passed as dealer that bid would be an artificial forcing spade raise, but by a passed hand it's natural. He has a balanced 11 or 12 points.

I'm certainly going to bid a game, but I doubt we have a slam. I suppose it's possible if North has little wasted heart strength opposite my singleton ace. If his hand is

> ♠ J 2 ♥ J 9 5 4 ♦ A J 7 3 ♣ A J 5,

6♠ would have about a 50-50 chance, but I'd be giving him perfect cards, and my partners never have exactly the right hand. I'm giving up on slam. It's matchpoints, after all, and if taking 12 tricks at 4♠ requires good play, +480 will give us a good result.

A pertinent question is whether we might do well at 3NT. Suppose North has

♠ 5 2 ♥ K Q 4 3 ♦ K 9 7 4 ♣ K 10 6.

Then we're probably off a spade and the minor-suit aces at 4♠ but might lose only the same three tricks at notrump.

I could stall by bidding 3♦ or 3♣, intending to shoot out a pass if North bids 3NT, but temporizing opposite a passed partner makes me nervous. If I bid 3♠, North might think I'm trying to sign off. (He shouldn't, but I'd rather win the event than an autopsy of the auction.) I reject 3♣ because some benefit may come from concealing my second suit from the defenders. I think a jump to 4♠ is practical, and that's the action I choose.

Everyone passes, and West leads the ♣4.

```
              ♠ Q 8 2
              ♥ J 10 7 2
              ♦ A 5
              ♣ A 10 7 5


              ♠ A K 10 9 4 3
              ♥ A
              ♦ Q 10
              ♣ Q 9 8 3
```

WEST	NORTH	EAST	SOUTH
	Pass	Pass	1♠
Pass	2NT	Pass	4♠
All Pass			

North's jump to 2NT was reasonable. As a passed hand, he had an awkward call. Some players might have raised to 3♠ or risked a "semi-forcing" 1NT response or a natural 2♣ response. In many partnerships North could use the Drury convention.

6♠ would have been a decent slam, but I'm satisfied to play where I am. I don't like this club lead, though, since it may be a singleton. I play low from dummy hopefully, and East takes the king and, to my relief, shifts to the ♥5 to my ace.

It looks like I have 11 tricks; I have no place to put my diamond loser. But I can see a positional squeeze against West if he has length in hearts plus the ♦K. I cash the ♠A to guard against a 4-0 split and lead to the ♠Q. East discards a heart. If East has heart length, I can't squeeze West, but I have another chance: I ruff a heart and take two more trumps, baring dummy's ♦A. East throws two diamonds. Then I cash the ♣Q—both defenders follow—go to the ♣A and lead the ♣10. East, who followed to the third club with his jack, looks unhappy and throws another diamond.

I suspect I have reached this position with three tricks left:

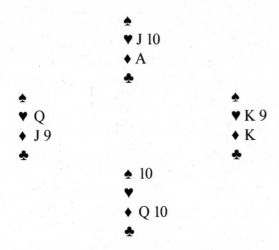

When I cash the ♦A, East's king falls, and my hand is high. East had no way out. If he had thrown another heart at the end, I could have ruffed a heart, making dummy high. The full deal:

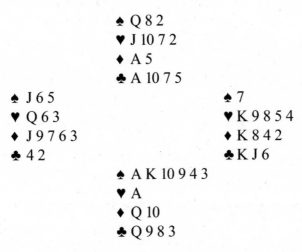

Our matchpoint result was good, and even +450 would have scored slightly above average. Most Souths played at 4♠, but the usual opening lead was a diamond. East got his ♦K, and some declarers later mis-guessed in clubs by taking two finesses through West and ended with only ten tricks.

In a Sectional Open Pairs, neither side is vulnerable, and as the dealer I pick up

♠ 8 4
♥ A Q J 10 5
♦ A 7 3
♣ A 6 2

This type of hand is hard to assess. The good five-card major suit and the side aces are promising, but there are also plenty of losers.

Many experts—I expect a majority—often open 1NT despite a five-card major. If I don't here, I'll have to underbid with 1NT over a 1♠ response. Nevertheless, a 1NT opening doesn't appeal to me. I'd rather have a hand with more secondary values such as

♠ Q 7 ♥ K J 10 6 4 ♦ A 10 6 ♣ K Q 8.

If North is broke, my actual hand may do poorly at notrump. Give North

♠ J 6 5 ♥ 8 3 2 ♦ Q J 8 6 ♣ 9 7 3,

and I might get clobbered at 1NT but take seven tricks at hearts.

Moreover, a 1NT opening may get me to an inferior fit. North might transfer me into 2♠ with

♠ Q J 6 5 2 ♥ K 6 4 ♦ 8 4 ♣ 8 7 3.

I think I'll take my chances and start with 1♥. I can handle any response except 1♠—but of course that is what North responds.

The opponents pass, and I rebid 1NT, hoping we don't miss a game. (A 2♥ rebid would suggest a six-card suit, but to rebid 2♥ here, treating that suit as a six-carder, would be acceptable.) North next bids 2♥. He must have true heart support, but with a weak hand and heart support he'd have raised to 2♥ at his first turn, confirming a fit and limiting his strength promptly. I expect a hand worth 10 or 11 points, and in that case, my bid is 4♥.

Everyone passes, and West leads the ♣K. I hope I haven't misjudged North's bidding.

```
              ♠ A Q 6 5 2
              ♥ K 8 3
              ♦ 10 5 2
              ♣ 7 3


              ♠ 8 4
              ♥ A Q J 10 5
              ♦ A 7 3
              ♣ A 6 2
```

WEST	NORTH	EAST	SOUTH
			1♥
Pass	1♠	Pass	1NT
Pass	2♥	Pass	4♥
All Pass			

North thought he was too heavy to raise to 2♥. If his ♦10 had been the king, he'd have jumped to 3♥, forcing, over my 1NT.

I win the first club. It's not the time to duck since a diamond shift might be fatal. I count eight tricks: five trumps plus three side aces. If the spade finesse wins, I can ruff a club in dummy for my tenth trick; otherwise, I must set up dummy's spades. I cash the ♥Q at the second trick and next try a spade to the queen. East takes the king and returns a club, and West wins and leads a third high club.

I need a 3-3 spade break, but even then I must draw trumps ending with the king. If I ruff this third club, my late entry to dummy will disappear. I pitch a diamond from dummy instead. West then shifts to a diamond—he can't gain by leading another club—and I win and cash the ♥J. When both defenders follow suit, I lead to the ♠A and ruff a spade high. The defenders politely follow again, and I can draw the missing trump with the king and take the good spades. The full deal:

```
              ♠ A Q 6 5 2
              ♥ K 8 3
              ♦ 10 5 2
              ♣ 7 3
♠ 10 9 3                        ♠ K J 7
♥ 9 6 2                         ♥ 7 4
♦ Q 9 6                         ♦ K J 8 4
♣ K Q J 4                       ♣ 10 9 8 5
              ♠ 8 4
              ♥ A Q J 10 5
              ♦ A 7 3
              ♣ A 6 2
```

At many tables, South opened 1NT, and North transferred to spades and bid 3NT next. The heart fit was lost, which proved costly. West led the ♣K, and though declarer had eight tricks, he couldn't set up an extra spade in time to make the contract.

One deal proves nothing, and I'm still a believer in opening 1NT on many hands with 2-5-3-3 pattern. Nevertheless, using your judgment is permitted.

As I See It

The Luck Factor

Luck is a factor at bridge. If you don't like it, you may as well take up bowling or basket weaving. Actually, one of the game's little pleasures is getting to complain about a horrible piece of luck and commiserating with other players who may have been even unluckier.

Players on the internet had to contend with this IMP deal:

```
Dlr: North          ♠ 10 9 6 5 4 2
Vul: N-S            ♥ 10 7
                    ♦ Q
                    ♣ 9 7 4 3
    ♠ J 8 7                        ♠ A K Q
    ♥ Q 3                          ♥ A K 9 8 5 2
    ♦ A K 10 7 6 5 3               ♦ 9 8
    ♣ 10                           ♣ A 5
                    ♠ 3
                    ♥ J 6 4
                    ♦ J 4 2
                    ♣ K Q J 8 6 2
```

It was a good grand slam, but many of the 40-odd East-Wests who played the deal languished at game. Sometimes North-South ignored the vulnerability and disrupted the auction effectively. More often, East or West simply failed to convey his trick-taking power. At several tables, the game-forcing 2/1 style came to grief. West responded 1NT to a 1♥ opening, describing his hand perfectly. East rebid 4♥, describing his, and the rest was silence.

Even when West responded 2♦, some auctions foundered. One East-West using 2/1 bid as follows: 1♥, 2♦-2♥, 3♦-3♠, 4♥. It was the old story: neither player ever made a value bid.

Most of the successful auctions—those that got as high as 6♥—began with 2♣. Indeed, East's hand looks like a 2♣ opener to me. East has nine playing tricks and five defensive tricks.

I heard about the deal from a player who was thoroughly disgusted at what had happened to him. He was East, and the bidding was

WEST	NORTH	EAST	SOUTH
	Pass	1♥	Pass
2♦	Pass	3♥	Pass
4NT	Pass	5♣	Dbl
5♦	Pass	6♥	All Pass

South, not knowing East-West had all the aces, led the ♠3!

East won, cashed the ♣A, ruffed his losing club in dummy and took the ♥Q. He then led a spade, intending to draw trumps and claim, and the next sound heard was "Oops." South ruffed and led a diamond, and East suffered a diamond ruff and another spade ruff. He was down two when drawing trumps would have made the contract. Unlucky!

One cannot say East misplayed. He runs into a ruff if spades break 6-1 (only a 6 percent chance though greater after the opening lead) but has a chance even then. To try to draw trumps at the second trick wins if trumps break 3-2, or if North has Hx, xx, or H in diamonds, in all at least 84%. In truth, East was fixed up by South's remarkable opening lead. After the ♣K opening lead, East would easily take 13 tricks.

It could have been worse, friend. At one table, East-West rolled into 7♥, and South led the ♣K. East-West were headed for a deserved 13-IMP gain—until East handled the play thus: ♣A, ♥Q(!), ♠A, club ruff, spade, Oops! East went down three and couldn't even complain about bad luck.

Pick Your Poison

We all know how elusive killing opening leads are. Players sometime try to give themselves an edge by leading an ace "to see dummy." What they may see instead is what lead would have been better. Besides, you get to see dummy no matter what you lead, and quite often you can't tell how a lead will turn out even after the dummy appears.

Suppose you're West in a strong IMP game and hold

♠ Q 10 3
♥ 10 4
♦ 10 6 4 3
♣ J 10 7 4

WEST	NORTH	EAST	SOUTH
			1♠
Pass	1NT	Pass	3♥
Pass	3♠	Pass	4♣
Pass	4♠	All Pass	

Pick your poison. (At least you don't have an ace.)

The full deal was:

Dlr: South
Vul: Both

```
                    ♠ 8 6
                    ♥ 5 3
                    ♦ A K J 8 7 2
                    ♣ 9 8 6
    ♠ Q 10 3                        ♠ 9 7 2
    ♥ 10 4                          ♥ Q 9 7 6
    ♦ 10 6 4 3                      ♦ Q 9 5
    ♣ J 10 7 4                      ♣ K Q 2
                    ♠ A K J 5 4
                    ♥ A K J 8 2
                    ♦ —
                    ♣ A 5 3
```

WEST	NORTH	EAST	SOUTH
			1♠
Pass	1NT	Pass	3♥
Pass	3♠	Pass	4♣
Pass	4♠	All Pass	

Credit North-South with a disciplined stop at game. After South's shape-showing 4♣ bid, North knew his diamond honors were not what partner needed.

When I watched the deal, West led the ♣J, reasonably enough. South took the ace and cranked out the ♥AK and another heart. West had to ruff in with the ten; otherwise, South would reach dummy and discard clubs on the high diamonds. Dummy threw a club.

West then led another club to East's queen. When a trump came back, South took the ace, ruffed a club and threw hearts on the ♦AK. He ruffed a diamond, cashed the ♠K to drop the queen, and claimed 11 tricks.

A trump shift by West at the fifth trick wouldn't help. South would win and lead a fourth heart, and though West could ruff in with the ♠Q, South would pitch dummy's last club and lose no more tricks. As the play went, however, East could have saved the overtrick by giving West another heart overruff.

I can reason out the best opening lead on this deal—perhaps not before or immediately after seeing the dummy, but certainly not long thereafter.

North's bidding suggests a doubleton spade and probably a doubleton heart (since with three-card heart support he might have tried 4♥ over 4♣). His most likely pattern is 2-2-5-4 or 2-2-6-3; and since he signed off when South issued a mild slam try, North's values are probably in diamonds. South, meanwhile, is surely 5-5-0-3 or 5-4-0-4.

The trumps are breaking well for declarer, and if East has nothing in hearts, 4♠ is surely impregnable; South was willing to investigate slam, remember. The defenders' best chance is to stop heart ruffs and hope to deprive South of any diamond tricks dummy can offer.

If West leads a low trump(!), he won't have a sure thing when he sees dummy, but he'll have hope. South could take ten tricks in theory, but in practice he will win with the jack and try three rounds of hearts. West will ruff in with the ten and return the ♠Q, stranding South with a heart and two clubs to lose.

Winning the Post-mortem

One of the recurring characters in my syndicated column is the dreaded "Grapefruit," he of the acid-tipped disposition, who is constantly telling his partners that if they were any dumber, they'd need to be watered twice a week. Grapefruit is the reflection of real-life players who would rather boost their ego by winning the post-mortem, not the event.

This deal arose in an all-expert team game:

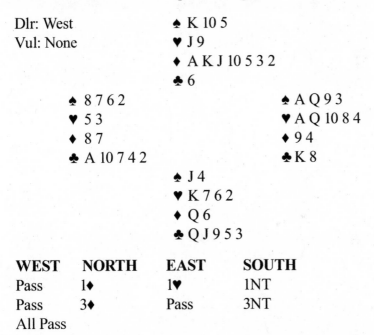

```
Dlr: West          ♠ K 10 5
Vul: None          ♥ J 9
                   ♦ A K J 10 5 3 2
                   ♣ 6
        ♠ 8 7 6 2              ♠ A Q 9 3
        ♥ 5 3                  ♥ A Q 10 8 4
        ♦ 8 7                  ♦ 9 4
        ♣ A 10 7 4 2           ♣ K 8
                   ♠ J 4
                   ♥ K 7 6 2
                   ♦ Q 6
                   ♣ Q J 9 5 3
```

WEST	NORTH	EAST	SOUTH
Pass	1♦	1♥	1NT
Pass	3♦	Pass	3NT
All Pass			

West knew dummy would have a flood of diamond tricks and South would hold at least one heart stopper. So West attacked with a club lead.

It's easy to construct a deal where this lead would have been a quick winner, but when the ♥J9 appeared in dummy, East was annoyed enough to begin planning the post-mortem instead of the defense. He put up the ♣K and, when it won, returned the ♣8. South offered his jack, and West pondered ... and played low.

South threw a spade from dummy and raced off seven diamonds, putting the East hand through the meat-grinder. In the end, South had no trouble taking his ninth trick with the ♥K.

The post-mortem commenced without delay:

East typed, "Pd, why can't you just lead my suit?"

West typed, "Pd, if you want the lead that bad, double 3NT."

East typed, "I have to risk a double to get my suit led? You still beat it if you take the ♣A and shift to a spade. What did you think I had for my opening bid?"

West typed: "If you had the major-suit aces and three clubs, I must duck the second club."

East typed: "Cowboy."

West typed: "Moron."

And from there, the colloquy deteriorated.

If you're a Grapefruit, you expect your partner to be omniscient, and when he's not, you punish him during the play and roast him when it's over. But if you're a mature player—and more interested in winning—you make the best of adverse situations.

When East takes the ♣K, he must shift to ♥A, ♥Q. South will get his eighth trick with the ♥K, but if he lacks the ♣A, he can never get a ninth. East's actual club return gave West a problem; the heart shift would make it easy for him.

****

At My Club

Dlr: South
Vul: Both

	♠ A 7 4 2		
	♥ Q 10 7 5 4 2		
	♦ 5 4		
	♣ K		

♠ J		♠ K 10 9 8 3
♥ K 6		♥ J 9 3
♦ 10 8 7 3		♦ Q J 6
♣ A Q 9 8 4 2		♣ J 5

♠ Q 6 5	
♥ A 8	
♦ A K 9 2	
♣ 10 7 6 3	

WEST	NORTH	EAST	SOUTH
			1♦
2♣	2♥	Pass	2NT
Pass	3NT(!)	All Pass	

"Who's that playing with Minnie?" I asked Mabel, our club manager. Minnie Bottoms is our senior member. Her old bifocals make her mix up kings and jacks, usually to her opponents' chagrin.

"That's Minnie's baby sister, Lotta," Mabel replied. "She's only 79. She's here visiting."

A duplicate was in progress, and since the Bottoms sisters were about to go up against Cy the Cynic, I sat down to watch. Minnie usually makes mincemeat of Cy. Sure enough, Cy landed at a strange 3NT—North's raise was inexplicable—and Minnie, West, led the ♣8. Cy welcomed the appearance of dummy's king.

Lotta Bottoms also wore bifocals—held together with adhesive tape. She peered owlishly at dummy and followed with her jack. Cy then called for a heart from dummy.

"It's not your lead," Lotta murmured. "My king won."

"Oh boy," Cy groaned.

They got it straightened out, but when Cy played his ♥A, Minnie dumped her king! Eventually, Lotta got in with her jack and led her last club, and Minnie ran the clubs. Down two.

"Your sister defends like you, Minnie," Cy said resignedly, "only more so."

"All I did was signal high from a doubleton," Minnie quavered.

"And I know enough to cover an honor," Lotta snapped.

Cy threw up his hands in despair.

If East doesn't unload her ♣J, the clubs are blocked; if West doesn't throw her ♥K under the ace, she must win the next heart. Either way, Cy would be safe.

PART the SIXTH

Sit Beside Me

In a Sectional Swiss Teams, both sides are vulnerable, and I'm East with

♠ A Q 5
♥ A 5 2
♦ A J 7 3
♣ K 9 4

North, the dealer, passes, and it's my call. This type of hand troubles me. Our 1NT range is 15 to 17 points, and I have 18 with some prime values. I ought to open 1♦ and jump to 2NT over a major suit response, but I don't like my hand for notrump. It lacks "body": good intermediate cards. If I held

♠ A Q 9   ♥ A 10 5   ♦ A J 8 5   ♣ K 10 9.

I'd start with 1♦ without a qualm. As it is, I'll weasel and open 1NT.

South overcalls 2♥, natural. He has good hearts but limited high-card values. If he had

♠ 7 6   ♥ K Q J 10 8 6   ♦ K 4   ♣ A Q 6,

he could double 1NT for penalty.

West and North pass. I can reopen with a double. Since I sit underneath the heart bidder, a double would be for takeout. But my hand is still better for defense, and my partner's hand is unknown. I'd just as soon not force him to declare at 2♠ on a weak 4-3 fit. So despite my extra values, I pass.

West leads the ♦K, and when I see dummy, I think we're better off defending.

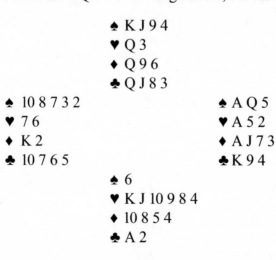

```
                        ♠ K J 9 4
                        ♥ Q 3
                        ♦ Q 9 6
                        ♣ Q J 8 3

                  N                 ♠ A Q 5
              W  -+- E              ♥ A 5 2
                  S                 ♦ A J 7 3
                                    ♣ K 9 4
```

WEST	NORTH	EAST	SOUTH
	Pass	1NT	2♥

All Pass

I signal with the ♦7, and West leads a second diamond to my jack. What next?

My partner has found a fine lead, but it won't pay off if I'm not careful. If I cash the ♦A next, I'll have no winning continuation. If I lead a fourth diamond, dummy will overruff West; if I shift to the ♥A and another heart to stop a ruff in dummy, South, who is marked with ♦10854, will draw trumps and concede a diamond to set up his ten.

So I lead a low diamond at the third trick, and West ruffs and leads a trump. I take the ace and lead another trump. South wins in dummy with the queen and leads the ♣Q for a winning finesse, but the full deal is

```
                        ♠ K J 9 4
                        ♥ Q 3
                        ♦ Q 9 6
                        ♣ Q J 8 3
    ♠ 10 8 7 3 2                       ♠ A Q 5
    ♥ 7 6                              ♥ A 5 2
    ♦ K 2                              ♦ A J 7 3
    ♣ 10 7 6 5                         ♣ K 9 4
                        ♠ 6
                        ♥ K J 10 9 8 4
                        ♦ 10 8 5 4
                        ♣ A 2
```

South still has two more losers—a diamond and a spade—and goes down one for +100 to us.

At the other table, East opened 1♦ in second seat, and South jumped to 2♥, preemptive. After two passes, East felt obliged to reopen with a double, and West's takeout to 2♠ ended the auction.

North led the ♥Q. West ducked, won the next heart, came to his ♦K, led a spade to the queen and cashed the ♠A. West next took the ♦A and ruffed a diamond, setting up dummy's jack, but then led a low club to the king. (He failed to infer that South probably had the ♣A since North, who passed as dealer, had shown the ♠KJ and both red queens.) The defense got three clubs and two trumps for down one, and we gained 5 IMPs.

If instead West leads a club to the nine, he's safe. Nor can North help the defense by splitting his club honors. Dummy's king loses to South's ace, but West will score a club trick and make his contract for +110 and a push.

I'm playing in an IMP League match at a friend's home, and both sides are vulnerable. As South, in third position, I pick up a battleship.

♠ A K Q
♥ 5
♦ A Q 6
♣ A K J 10 9 3

This is a fine 2♣ opening. I have about ten playing tricks opposite the worst hand my imagination can devise for my partner, and my defensive values are more than adequate.

When I hold a hand like this, it seems as if I never get to open 2♣ and enjoy a leisurely auction. My right-hand opponent invariably opens 4♥, and I end up guessing at the best contract. But this time, to my surprise, my partner opens 1♥.

A hand such as

♠ 6 5 4 ♥ A J 8 6 4 ♦ K J 4 ♣ Q 7

will make us laydown for 7NT, and that's not even an opening bid. But North could have

♠ J 4 3 ♥ A Q J 7 4 ♦ K J 4 ♣ 8 7,

and I'd need to pick up the clubs. It's tempting to trot out Blackwood, but I'd like to learn whether North has the ♣Q. It may not matter what my first response is, but I start with a jump-shift to 3♣ even though my suit isn't solid. (A player who jump-shifts should know what trumps will be or should have a strong balanced hand with which he'll bid notrump next. If I had a weaker hand such as

♠ A K Q ♥ 5 ♦ A Q 6 2 ♣ A J 8 5 3,

I'd respond 2♣ despite my 20 high-card points since the best trump suit would be in doubt and I'd need room to look for it.)

Over my 3♣, North surprises me again by jumping to 4♥. He should have a solid suit, and that's enough for me. I bid 7NT and expect to claim after the opening lead. Everyone passes, and West leads the ♠J.

```
          ♠ 8 5 3
          ♥ A K Q 10 9 6 3
          ♦ K 2
          ♣ 2

          ♠ A K Q
          ♥ 5
          ♦ A Q 6
          ♣ A K J 10 9 3
```

WEST	NORTH	EAST	SOUTH
	1♥	Pass	3♣
Pass	4♥	Pass	7NT
All Pass			

The grand slam isn't a claimer, but if everything works, I can make six overtricks. The hearts will come in more than 70% of the time; otherwise, I'll need the clubs.

A principle of dummy play is to wait to attack key suits, so I take the ♠A and cash the ♠KQ. East discards a diamond. Next I take the three top diamonds, and West pitches a spade. I know West had seven cards in spades and diamonds, and East had eight. Now it's time for the hearts, but when I cash the ♥AK, East discards a diamond. On the ♥Q he discards another diamond.

216

I have 11 top tricks — three spades, three hearts, three diamonds and two clubs — and need two more in clubs. I know East's shape was 2-1-6-4, so a winning club finesse won't help: I'll lose the last trick to the ♣Q. The only hope is to cash the ♣AK, hoping West has Q-x. And he does! This has been a deal of surprises.

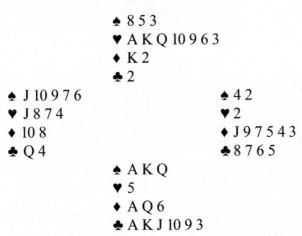

```
              ♠ 8 5 3
              ♥ A K Q 10 9 6 3
              ♦ K 2
              ♣ 2
  ♠ J 10 9 7 6            ♠ 4 2
  ♥ J 8 7 4               ♥ 2
  ♦ 10 8                  ♦ J 9 7 5 4 3
  ♣ Q 4                   ♣ 8 7 6 5
              ♠ A K Q
              ♥ 5
              ♦ A Q 6
              ♣ A K J 10 9 3
```

I hoped for a swing but didn't get one. At the other table, North-South reached 7♥. East led a diamond, and North, the declarer, took the king and cashed the ♥AK. When East discarded, declarer embarked on a coup: ♣A, club ruff, ♦A, club ruff, spade, club ruff, spade. With three tricks left, the position, with dummy (South) to lead, was

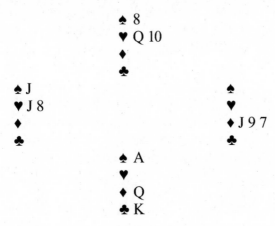

```
              ♠ 8
              ♥ Q 10
              ♦
              ♣
  ♠ J                      ♠
  ♥ J 8                    ♥
  ♦                        ♦ J 9 7
  ♣                        ♣
              ♠ A
              ♥
              ♦ Q
              ♣ K
```

West's trumps were trapped, and the deal was tied.

217

My partner in a Regional Open Pairs is as bold a bidder as I am conservative, but sometimes odd-couple partnerships excel because the players exert a moderating influence on each other. With both sides vulnerable, I am the dealer with:

♠ K 8 7 6 2
♥ 5 4 2
♦ A K 10 5 2
♣ —

I have no doubt that my partner would open this hand, as would many other players. The standard for opening bids seems to have gotten lighter and lighter. I wouldn't quarrel with opening 1♠ and I'd be tempted to open myself with better intermediates in spades. As it is, I stick to my style and pass. Overstating high-card values is a risk. If, for instance, I opened 1♠ and raised a 2♥ response to 3♥, wild horses wouldn't keep North out of 6♥ if he held

♠ Q 3 ♥ A K 9 6 3 ♦ J 4 ♣ A K J 3.

After two passes, my partner opens 1♣, and I respond 1♠. With two five-card suits, the normal practice is to bid the higher-ranking suit first. The opponents pass, and North leaps to 4♦, a "splinter bid." He shows slam interest, spade support and shortness in diamonds (usually a singleton).

I like my hand for slam. Although my ♦K isn't the greatest honor opposite North's shortness, it's a winner and will help me establish my long diamonds. Moreover, my fifth spade will take a trick. I cue-bid 5♦, and my partner replies 5♥.

A grand slam is possible, but I'm not going to speculate in a pairs event, especially since I don't totally trust my partner's bidding. If 13 tricks require good play or good luck, we'll get a good result for +1460. I settle for 6♠, and everyone passes. West leads the ♣J.

♠ A Q 5 4
♥ A J 7 6
♦ 7
♣ K Q 5 3

♠ K 8 7 6 2
♥ 5 4 2
♦ A K 10 5 2
♣ —

WEST	NORTH	EAST	SOUTH
	1♣	Pass	1♠
Pass	4♦	Pass	5♦
Pass	5♥	Pass	6♠
All Pass			

As I suspected, North overbid and 6♠ is high enough. His hand looks to me like a simple raise to 3♠, and his 5♥ cue-bid (although many players would have felt obliged to cue-bid) was lusty.

I call for the ♣Q, and East's ace covers. That's a help. Now I have a club winner in dummy, but I still have work to do. To make the slam I must set up the diamonds, presumably by ruffing twice in dummy.

Before I ruff the ♣A, I try to visualize the play. Suppose I ruff, cash the ♦A, ruff a diamond, ruff a club and ruff a diamond. If both defenders follow, I'll cash the ♠AQ, but if trumps break 3-1, I can't get back to my hand to draw the last trump without losing control. No good.

How about discarding a heart now instead of ruffing? That will cost nothing — I expect to lose one heart anyway — and I'll preserve an entry to my hand.

When I discard a heart, East ponders and leads the ♠3. I play low and take West's nine in dummy with the ace. I come to the ♦A, ruff a diamond, discard another heart on the ♣K, ruff a club and ruff a diamond. East-West follow suit, so I take the ♠Q. West discards, but I can cash the ♥A, ruff a heart, draw East's last trump and win the last two tricks with the ♦K and ♦10. The full deal:

```
              ♠ A Q 5 4
              ♥ A J 7 6
              ♦ 7
              ♣ K Q 5 3
  ♠ 9                        ♠ J 10 3
  ♥ Q 9                      ♥ K 10 8 3
  ♦ Q 9 6 4                  ♦ J 8 3
  ♣ J 10 9 6 4 2            ♣ A 8 7
              ♠ K 8 7 6 2
              ♥ 5 4 2
              ♦ A K 10 5 2
              ♣ —
```

In my experience, players often use splinter bids with high-card values that are too skimpy. They succumb to the lure of finding a perfect hand across the table. True, splinters are meant to locate distributional slams, but you must draw the high-card line somewhere. North would argue that his bid would help us reach a good slam if I held

♠ K 8 7 6 2 ♥ K 2 ♦ 10 5 2 ♣ A 4 2,

but if instead he merely raised to 3♠, I might make one slam try by cue-bidding 4♣.

As for the play: what a lesson on planning before playing to the first trick! If declarer ruffs the first club, the slam is unmakable.

In a Regional Swiss Teams, both sides are vulnerable, and as South I pick up a promising hand:

♠ A K 8 7 6 2
♥ 5
♦ Q J 8 3
♣ A 9

North, the dealer, opens 1♥, and I start my campaign with a 1♠ response. North rebids 2♣, and I try 2♦. It happens that I have a diamond suit, but I would also bid 2♦, giving North a chance to make a third descriptive bid, if my hand were

♠ A K 8 7 6 2 ♥ 5 ♦ A 8 3 ♣ A 9 4.

220

A jump to 3♠ wouldn't be forcing.

North next bids 2NT, and I continue with 3♠. I wouldn't bid this way with a weak hand or even with an average hand, so 3♠ is forcing and suggests a six-card suit. North raises to 4♠, and I must decide whether to go on.

So far North has promised no more than minimum values, but for all he knows, we've been looking for the best game. His hand may still be suited for slam. I expect he has 2-5-2-4 distribution, so slam won't be good if he holds

♠ Q 4 ♥ K Q 8 6 4 ♦ A 5 ♣ K 7 6 5;

but if he has the ♥A instead of the K-Q, 6♠ may be cold or at least a favorite.

My approach in possible slam auctions is, "When in doubt, make a try." It's wrong to mastermind and make a final decision too soon, so I consult partner with a 5♣ cue-bid. There is a danger, of course, that we may go down at the five level, but I think that's a risk worth taking.

North replies 5♥. My partnership's philosophy is that a cue-bid shows slam interest; North wouldn't cue-bid if he didn't like his hand. So I leap to 6♠, perhaps optimistically, and everyone passes. West leads the ♣5.

```
              ♠ Q 4
              ♥ A J 9 6 4
              ♦ K 2
              ♣ K 7 6 3

              ♠ A K 8 7 6 2
              ♥ 5
              ♦ Q J 8 3
              ♣ A 9
```

WEST	NORTH	EAST	SOUTH
	1♥	Pass	1♠
Pass	2♣	Pass	2♦
Pass	2NT	Pass	3♠
Pass	4♠	Pass	5♣
Pass	5♥	Pass	6♠
All Pass			

That's not a bad dummy. I don't mind North's bid of 2NT, though over 2♦ some Norths would have taken a 2♠ preference. Such a preference is often based on a doubleton honor. If North had good three-card support, he'd have raised directly to 2♠ or would have jumped to 3♠ over 2♦.

To make the slam I must assume that trumps will break 3-2, giving me 11 sure tricks: six spades, two clubs, two diamonds and a heart. The easy route to one more trick is to ruff a diamond in dummy. To set up a long heart I'd probably need not only a favorable heart break but more sure entries than dummy has.

I'd better keep the ♣A as an entry to my hand, so I win the first club with the king and lead the ♦K. Both defenders play low, so I try a diamond to my queen. West takes the ace and leads another club, and I take the ace and ruff my low diamond with dummy's low trump. Both defenders follow, so I cash the ♠Q and the ♥A, ruff a heart and take the ♣A. When East-West follow, I can draw the last trump and claim. The full deal:

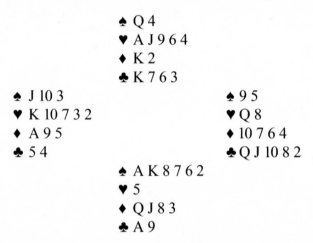

Taking 12 tricks seemed easy, but I'd probably go down if I win the opening lead in my hand.* The play would continue with a diamond to the king, a diamond to the queen and ace, a club return to dummy's king, the ♥A, a heart ruff, a diamond ruff and the ♠Q. But then I'd be stuck in dummy. If I tried to come back with a club ruff, West would overruff. If instead I led a heart, East would uppercut effectively with the ♠9.

---

*A guard squeeze (a rare animal) could still produce 12 tricks.

I anticipated a swing, and sure enough, at the other table my teammate in the West led a trump against 6♠. South took the queen and led the ♦K, and West won and led another trump, stopping the diamond ruff in dummy.

It looked as if South had only 11 tricks, but he drew West's last trump, cashed the ♦QJ, ran some more trumps and led to the ♥A in this position:

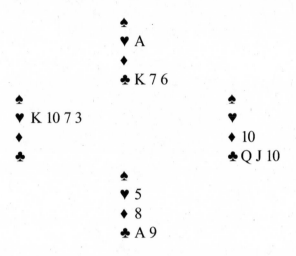

```
                    ♠
                    ♥ A
                    ♦
                    ♣ K 7 6
    ♠                               ♠
    ♥ K 10 7 3                      ♥
    ♦                               ♦ 10
    ♣                               ♣ Q J 10
                    ♠
                    ♥ 5
                    ♦ 8
                    ♣ A 9
```

East was squeezed in the minors, and the slam was made for a push.

As I See It

Three Against One

At IMPs, with your side vulnerable, you hold as South:

♠ A K 10 3
♥ Q 3
♦ 10 8 6 4
♣ A 8 5

North deals and opens 2♦, probably a weak two-bid in a major suit. East passes. What is your call?

Suppose you settle for a conversion to 2♥. After two passes, East reopens with 2♠. What is your call?

Suppose you pass, West tries 2NT and you hear two more passes. What is your call?

I was reading an account of a U.S. Trials in a back issue of The Bridge World, and the author, a well known theorist, displayed a condescending attitude toward the approach to weak two-bids employed by the writer and editor Matthew Granovetter. On one deal, Matt opened 2♥ on

♠ 10 3 2
♥ K Q J 8 6 3
♦ 6
♣ A 7 5

and the author remarked that it "looked more like a super-weak strong two-bid than a weak two-bid." He slyly deprecated other actions that reflected Matthew's sound style: for instance, a 2♦ opening on

♠ 10 8 7
♥ A
♦ K J 10 9 5 4
♣ Q 5 2

(On that deal, Matthew went plus. His counterpart at the other table opened 1♦, and partner, with 12 high-card points, forced to game and went down 300 at 3NT. Gee, imagine that.)

That was in 2001, and I suspect that matters on the weak two-bid front are worse now. Opening one-bids have become lighter and lighter, pushing the range for a weak two-bid into the nether regions. Moreover, the modern emphasis on obstruction has turned the weak two-bid into an undisciplined action. Authorities write — and an appearance in the pages of The Bridge World or Bulletin gives legitimacy to their views — that it's all but mandatory to open 2♠ despite a side void, or despite holding four good hearts, or despite a trashy suit. Impressionable players treat what they read as fact, not opinion.

Some players justify such actions on the theory that they get two-to-one odds. They have two opponents to fool but only one partner. Personally, I think the odds are one-to-three. I detest catapulting my partner into the unknown. Is it so terrible to keep your weak two-bids within disciplined limits?

I watched the deal below in a strong IMP game.

Dlr: North
Vul: N-S

	♠ 6 4	
	♥ A J 8 5 4 2	
	♦ Q 9 7 3	
	♣ 6	
♠ 9 8		♠ Q J 7 5 2
♥ K 10 9		♥ 7 6
♦ A J 5		♦ K 2
♣ Q 10 9 7 2		♣ K J 4 3
	♠ A K 10 3	
	♥ Q 3	
	♦ 10 8 6 4	
	♣ A 8 5	

WEST	NORTH	EAST	SOUTH
	2♦ (1)	Pass	2♥(!)
Pass	Pass	2♠	Pass(!)
2NT	Pass	Pass	3♥(!!)
All Pass			

(1) usually a weak two-bid in a major suit

South's actions strike me as incomprehensible. South so distrusted his partner's weak two-bid (vulnerable against not!) that he refused to even try for game. North's hand was full of holes, yet 4♥ had a play. If North had held a slightly better hand such as 64,AK8542,J973,6 or 64,AJ10542,K973,6, a vulnerable game would have been well worth attempting.

Then when the opponents unwisely balanced, South let them off the hook. Both 2♠ and 2NT would have been mauled with best defense. The trouble was that South wasn't sure what North had. If North had held a fashionable modern weak two-bid, I suppose South couldn't be sure of beating a game.

True, East-West probably would take eight tricks at clubs—which raises the old question of whether a player should double what's in front of his nose and worry later. The question has no answer, but my tendency has been to give fate a chance and double unless the risk of a successful run-out is particularly obvious.

The gingerly bid 3♥ contract made four when East-West failed to find their diamond ruff. I suppose North-South were satisfied with their +170, which beat the "par" result on the deal. I wouldn't have been.

Control Freaks

As West, neither side vulnerable, you hold

♠ A J 6 3
♥ K Q 9 4 2
♦ 10
♣ 10 6 2

Suppose I put a noose around your neck and make you open 1♥. (Nowadays, many players would supply their own noose.) East responds

2NT, a forcing heart raise. Despite your minimum, you must bid 3♦, systemically showing a singleton diamond. Partner then bids 3♥. What is your next action?

Say instead that you pass as dealer, East opens 1♥ and South jumps to 2NT, "Unusual." You try 4♦, showing a big heart fit and diamond shortness. North saves at 5♣, your partner bids 5♥ and South passes. Are you through?

One more question. Your partner opens 1♥. Which of these 10-HCP hands do you prefer?

♠ A K 6 3		♠ A J 6 3
♥ K 9 8 4 2	or	♥ K Q 9 4 2
♦ 10		♦ 10
♣ 10 6 2		♣ 10 6 2

A controversial aspect of cue-bidding to slam, and one treated elsewhere in this book, is whether cue-bids below game should be cooperative or constructive. Suppose you hold

♠ J 9 6 3
♥ A J 6
♦ Q 8 2
♣ K Q 7

You open 1♣ and raise partner's 1♠ response to 2♠. He jumps to 4♦, a natural try for slam. You have only one ace and one king and no high honor in trumps, and your pattern is as flat as a pancake. Must you show your ace by cue-bidding 4♥ or may you sign off at 4♠?

I believe a majority of experts would bid 4♥. The minority view, with which I concur, is that a cue-bid shows slam interest, and mandatory cue-bids dilute the major advantage of cue-bidding: the chance for either partner to exercise judgment.

♠ A K 10 7 5 4	♠ J 9 6 3
♥ 8 2	♥ A J 6
♦ A K J 5	♦ Q 8 2
♣ 5	♣ K Q 7

WEST	EAST
	1 ♣
1 ♠	2 ♠
4 ♦	4 ♥
4 NT	5 ♦
6 ♠	

6♠ is only fair, always down with a heart opening lead and needing to pick up the trumps otherwise. After East cue-bid 4♥, I can't blame West for driving to slam. The problem with cue-bidding on East's hand is psychological. It's easy to say that 4♥ is forced and shows no extra strength, but in practice West will be more likely to bid a lot if he hears East cue-bid. The auction should be

WEST	EAST
	1 ♣
1 ♠	2 ♠
4 ♦	4 ♠
5 ♦	5 ♥
5 ♠	Pass

I watched the deal below in a strong IMP game.

Dlr: West
Vul: None

```
                    ♠ K 10 8 7 4
                    ♥ 8 3
                    ♦ 9 5 4
                    ♣ Q 5 4
    ♠ A J 6 3                        ♠ 5 2
    ♥ K Q 9 4 2                      ♥ A 10 7 6 5
    ♦ 10                             ♦ A J 8 3
    ♣ 10 6 2                         ♣ A 9
                    ♠ Q 9
                    ♥ J
                    ♦ K Q 7 6 2
                    ♣ K J 8 7 3
```

WEST	NORTH	EAST	SOUTH
1♥	Pass	2NT	Pass
3♦	Pass	3♥	Pass
3♠	Pass	4♣	Pass
4♥	Pass	6♥	All Pass

229

To open as West wouldn't have occurred to me, but such is the progressive style. I will argue, however, with anyone who thinks West must cue-bid 3♠, and I will argue with anyone who thinks East was wrong to bid 6♥ when West suggested slam (well, didn't he?) by cue-bidding.

At most tables, West didn't open. East started with 1♥, and many East-Wests had to cope with minor-suit competition by North-South. The usual result was +450, though a few North-Souths saved at five of a minor and took penalties ranging from -500 to -1100. At one table the auction was

WEST	NORTH	EAST	SOUTH
Pass	Pass	1♥	2NT
4♦	5♣	5♥	Pass
6♥	All Pass		

No doubt East should have doubled 5♣ since he could visualize a defense starting with the ♦A and a diamond ruff, a heart to the ace and another diamond ruff. He was punished for competing with 5♥ when West forgot that he had shown his hand by bidding 4♦. Moreover, West's hand wasn't as strong as its high-card count suggested since the ♥Q would often be a wasted honor. If West's ♥Q and ♠J were the ♠K, 6♥ would be cold.

The dubious heart slam was reached at yet another table, and South led the ♦K. East took the ace, drew trumps and led a low spade from dummy. North unwisely put up his king, after which East emerged with 12 tricks. So maybe it wasn't such a bad slam after all.

To Bee Or Not To Bee

"Everybody wants ta get inta da act."—Jimmy Durante.

Here's a problem in dummy play:

Dlr: South
Vul: None

♠ 9 7 6
♥ 10 7 6 4
♦ 9 7 5
♣ J 10 8

♠ A K
♥ A
♦ A K 8 3
♣ A K 9 7 6 5

With a minimum of encouragement from North, you arrive at 6♣, and West leads the ♦Q. You win with the ace and cash the ♣A, and the queen falls at your left. That's one problem solved, but how do you continue?

Quite a few declarers confidently laid down the ♦K, expecting to concede a diamond and ruff a diamond in dummy if necessary. East shattered that plan by ruffing the ♦K, and South lost a diamond later and went down.

No doubt you displayed good technique by going to dummy with a trump to lead the second diamond toward your hand. If East ruffed, he'd only be ruffing your diamond loser, and you could win the trump return and claim. If instead East discarded, you'd take the ♦K, lose a diamond and ruff your last diamond with the ♣J.

This line of play would lose if West started with the singleton queen in both minors or with the doubleton ♦Q (East would win the third diamond and lead a third round of trumps, stopping the ruff in dummy), but the odds seem to favor it. The full deal:

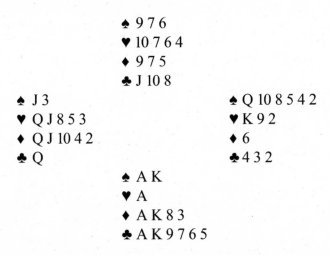

```
              ♠ 9 7 6
              ♥ 10 7 6 4
              ♦ 9 7 5
              ♣ J 10 8
♠ J 3                          ♠ Q 10 8 5 4 2
♥ Q J 8 5 3                    ♥ K 9 2
♦ Q J 10 4 2                   ♦ 6
♣ Q                            ♣ 4 3 2
              ♠ A K
              ♥ A
              ♦ A K 8 3
              ♣ A K 9 7 6 5
```

Maybe you'd like to know more about the bidding. At many tables, East-West remained silent, but — and now it's time to release the feline from the bag — some Wests couldn't resist getting into act. At one table, for instance, this was the auction:

WEST	NORTH	EAST	SOUTH
			2♣
2♥	Pass	Pass	3♣
3♦	Pass	3♥	Pass
Pass	4♣	Pass	6♣
All Pass			

What West thought he had to gain by acting with his junk pile is a mystery. His bidding wasn't especially obstructive, and finding a paying sacrifice was unlikely when he was looking at all those losers. The most likely effect of West's bidding was to help South play the hand. But West was one of the Busy Bees, as Matthew and Pamela Granovetter call them; a Busy Bee buzzes around with a lot of active bidding that confirms his presence at the table but serves no other purpose.

West led the ♦Q again, and this time the auction had lit a fire under declarer. Having been warned about the diamond position, South found the winning line of play without difficulty.*

If you want ta get inta da act, have a reason.

*Declarer can also make 6♣ by running his trumps and catching West in a squeeze-and-endplay.

At My Club

Dlr: South		♠ 5	
Vul: Both		♥ 8 6 4 3	
		♦ A K Q 10 7 4 3	
		♣ 5	

♠ K 10 8 6 2	♠ Q J 7 4
♥ K Q 9 7	♥ 10
♦ 9	♦ J 6 5
♣ K 9 3	♣ Q 10 8 7 4

	♠ A 9 3
	♥ A J 5 2
	♦ 8 2
	♣ A J 6 2

WEST	NORTH	EAST	SOUTH
			1♣
1♠	2♦	3♠	Pass
Pass	4♦	Pass	4♥
All Pass			

I was in the club lounge when I heard a ruckus erupt in the penny Chicago game. A kibitzer came in, shaking his head.

"That Grapefruit reminds me of the nun who belonged to an order with a vow of silence," he sighed. "She had permission to speak two words every ten years. Her first two were `hard bed,' and the Mother Superior was sympathetic. Ten years later, the nun said `cold food,' and Mother sighed and promised to improve the cuisine. Ten years passed, and the nun spoke again: `I quit.'

"'I don't wonder,' growled the Mother Superior. 'All you've done since you've been here is gripe'."

Grapefruit, our member who owns and operates an acid disposition, was North and was anything but silent after West led a spade against 4♥, and South took the ♠A and led a low trump. South planned to cash the ace later and then run the diamonds, losing two trumps but nothing else.

East won and led another spade. When South ruffed in dummy and led a second trump, East showed out, and the hand collapsed. South took the ace, ruffed his last spade in dummy and started the diamonds, but West ruffed the second diamond. South went down three, and Grapefruit snarled that if South were an elevator operator, he couldn't remember his route.

Since South had no side-suit losers, he could afford to lose three trumps. At the second trick South must cash the ♥A but then abandon trumps forever. He starts the diamonds, and West gets only his three trumps.

It'd be nice if Grapefruit took a vow of silence, but we're not optimistic.

Sit Beside Me

In the opening round of a Regional Knockout Teams, only my side is vulnerable, and I'm South, in fourth position, with

♠ A Q 10 9 6
♥ A Q 8
♦ Q 10 3
♣ 7 4

I hear three passes and open 1♠. West, a passed hand, doubles for takeout, and my partner redoubles. East passes, and so do I; I have nothing special to say. North may have one of many types of hands. He may intend to double anything he hears; he may plan to bid notrump; he may have spade support. I give him the courtesy of the road.

West runs to 1NT. He doesn't have a long suit to bid and is hoping East will bid something. If we double 1NT and East doesn't act, West may redouble, forcing his partner to choose a port in the storm.

But over 1NT, my partner jumps to 3♠. His redouble promised 10 or more high-card points, so if he had bid only 2♠, he'd have invited game. If he weren't a passed hand, his 3♠ would be forcing. As it is, I expect him to have a maximum pass with great spade support.

I don't like my hand much. If North doesn't have the ♥K, West probably has it, and my queen may be worthless. Still, I can't afford to miss a decent vulnerable game at IMPs. I bid 4♠, and everyone passes. West huddles and leads a trump.

♠ K J 8 7 3
♥ 7 4
♦ K 7
♣ K J 5 3

♠ A Q 10 9 6
♥ A Q 8
♦ Q 10 3
♣ 7 4

WEST	NORTH	EAST	SOUTH
Pass	Pass	Pass	1♠
Dbl	Redbl	Pass	Pass
1NT	3♠	Pass	4♠
All Pass			

I'm surprised North didn't bid 4♠ himself. He'd probably say he has seen me play the dummy before. West has found a safe opening lead, and ten tricks will require some guessing. I draw trumps, West discarding a diamond, and lead a diamond to the king, winning, and a diamond to my ten. West wins with the jack, alas, and shifts to the ♣2, and I must take a position in clubs. My game may be on the line: I don't expect the heart finesse to win.

Come to think of it, I should assume that the heart finesse will lose. If it wins, the contract is safe. If I give West the ♥K, what else can he have? He has shown the ♦AJ and may have the ♥J. If he had the ♣A, he'd probably have opened the bidding. So I play the ♣J, and East takes the ace. The heart finesse fails later, but I lose only a heart, a club and a diamond. The full deal is:

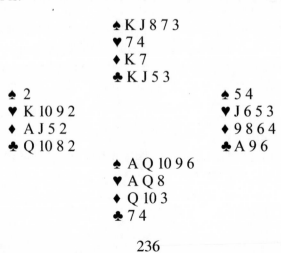

♠ K J 8 7 3
♥ 7 4
♦ K 7
♣ K J 5 3

♠ 2
♥ K 10 9 2
♦ A J 5 2
♣ Q 10 8 2

♠ 5 4
♥ J 6 5 3
♦ 9 8 6 4
♣ A 9 6

♠ A Q 10 9 6
♥ A Q 8
♦ Q 10 3
♣ 7 4

The play was an example of a "second-degree assumption." You assume the cards lie a certain way—so that your contract can be assured or is at risk—and follow the consequences of your assumption. If my club finesse with the jack lost to the queen and West turned up with the ♣A, the heart finesse would win.

Most players would have tried that passed-hand double as West, but light intervention can lose by giving declarer a roadmap in the play. Since West didn't have spades, he wasn't likely to buy the contract opposite a passed hand. True, he might have found a good sacrifice, but this time he'd have done well to keep silent. We'd still have reached 4♠, but whether I'd have made it, I can't say.

In a Regional Knockout event with a random draw, we face one of the less experienced teams in the first round. After three flat boards, I as South pick up

♠ A K J 7 5 2
♥ A 5 3
♦ A 9 4
♣ 4

Only our side is vulnerable, and I hear three passes. I open 1♠, West overcalls 2♣, my partner raises to 2♠ and East competes with 3♣.

The opponents may have a good save at 5♣, but I can't afford to try to deter them with any devious tactics – such as "walking" my hand by bidding only 3♠. I leap to 4♠, and after two more passes East tries 5♣.

We can probably beat them a couple — maybe more — but if we collect only 300 when 5♠ is cold, we risk an 8-IMP loss. Whether 5♠ will make, I have no idea. If I had to guess, I'd say no and would double, but I have a partner at the table. I pass – forcing since the opponents have clearly sacrificed against our game. If North wants to double 5♣, fine; if he pushes on to 5♠, I'll expect to have a play for it.

My partner thinks for a long time before bidding 5♠. Everyone passes, West leads the ♣A, and partner puts down a borderline dummy.

"If you don't make it," he says gloomily, "it's my fault."

237

♠ 10 9 6 3
♥ K 4
♦ K J 5 2
♣ 9 6 3

♠ A K J 7 5 2
♥ A 5 3
♦ A 9 4
♣ 4

WEST	NORTH	EAST	SOUTH
Pass	Pass	Pass	1♠
2♣	2♠	3♣	4♠
Pass	Pass	5♣	Pass
Pass	5♠	All Pass	

North indeed had a close decision. His four trumps and no wasted club honors argued for bidding, and he was sure I had a singleton club to pass 5♣ around. His minimum high-card strength suggested doubling. Let's see if I can "pick him up."

West continues with the ♣K, and I ruff. I lead the ♠A, not confidently, and I'm not surprised when East discards. If we had a spade trick to cash, their save wouldn't have been too attractive. Since I have a trump to lose, all depends on the diamonds.

I cash the ♠K and play three rounds of hearts, ruffing in dummy. West follows low twice, then drops the queen. Now I know a finesse with the ♦J can't win: West, who passed as dealer and has shown the ♣AK and both major-suit queens, can't have the ♦Q. But I can place him with 3-3-2-5 distribution, so I still have hope. I lead to the ♦K and return the ♦J. East plays low, and the jack wins as West's ten falls. I'm fortunate to claim 11 tricks, losing a trump. The full deal:

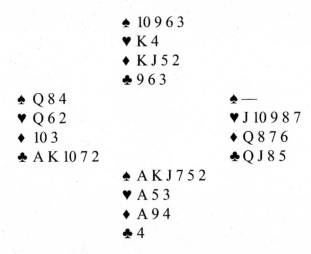

```
              ♠ 10 9 6 3
              ♥ K 4
              ♦ K J 5 2
              ♣ 9 6 3
♠ Q 8 4                      ♠ —
♥ Q 6 2                      ♥ J 10 9 8 7
♦ 10 3                       ♦ Q 8 7 6
♣ A K 10 7 2                 ♣ Q J 8 5
              ♠ A K J 7 5 2
              ♥ A 5 3
              ♦ A 9 4
              ♣ 4
```

At the other table, the auction started the same way, but our East put on the pressure by leaping to 5♣ directly. Since South had yet to show strength, he felt he had to take a position instead of passing to partner, and his double was understandable.

North led the ♠10, and our declarer ruffed in dummy and started the hearts. South jumped up with the ace and shifted to a trump, and West won and continued with the ♥Q to North's king. The defense then took the high diamonds but misjudged by missing their heart ruff. So West was -300 and East's advance save was worth 8 IMPs.

I'm playing in a club duplicate with an aspiring player who doesn't know how rusty I am. Writing is different from playing: Table presence, focus and judgment suffer unless you stay sharp through practice. Nevertheless, we're having a pleasant game, and toward the end, having done nothing disgraceful so far, I pick up

```
              ♠ A K Q 8 5 3
              ♥ K J 5
              ♦ 4
              ♣ Q 9 6
```

Only our side is vulnerable, and as South, the dealer, I open 1♠. West passes, my partner responds 2NT, natural and forcing, and East leaps preemptively to 4♣. When he puts his "Stop" card back in the bidding box, I wait another few seconds and bid 4♠. At IMPs I might consider taking the money and doubling 4♣. Since my partner has something in clubs, we'd probably beat it two or three. But at matchpoints I can't accept +300 or +500 when we can be +620 or more at 4♠.

I expect the auction to end, but my partner ponders and reaches for a card that isn't green. 6♠. Well, oops. I hope he doesn't think I have a huge hand just because I rebid my stout spades.

West leads the ♥A, and when dummy appears, I see we're at a top-or-bottom contract.

♠ J 10 2
♥ Q 10 6
♦ A K 9 5
♣ A 7 3

♠ A K Q 8 5 3
♥ K J 5
♦ 4
♣ Q 9 6

WEST	NORTH	EAST	SOUTH
			1♠
Pass	2NT	4♣	4♠
Pass	6♠(!)	All Pass	

"I hope you've got a singleton club," my partner says. I don't reply. It won't pay to give the opponents more of an edge than the bidding has already given them.

East follows with the ♥4, and West leads another heart. I play low from dummy, and East discards a high club. What about that! He had 12 minor-suit cards. I guess we'd have beaten 4♣ doubled only 300,* but I'd rather be there than at this wild slam.

I take the ♥K and realize that my only chance is to squeeze East. I have 11 tricks – six spades, two hearts, two diamonds and a club. A simple squeeze won't work: West has three diamonds, and if one of them is higher than dummy's nine, West can guard diamonds. But I see an alternative. I win the second heart with the king and run five trumps, pitching two clubs from dummy. Next comes a heart to the queen, leaving this position:

*Actually, best defense would beat it 500.

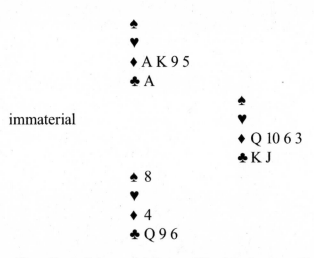

♠
♥
♦ A K 9 5
♣ A

immaterial

♠
♥
♦ Q 10 6 3
♣ K J

♠ 8
♥
♦ 4
♣ Q 9 6

East, still to discard, has no defense. If he blanks the ♣K, I'll cash the ♣A and my clubs will be good; if he comes down to three diamonds, I'll take the ♦AK and ruff a diamond, and dummy will be good. Since I know his distribution, he can't discard to fool me. The full deal:

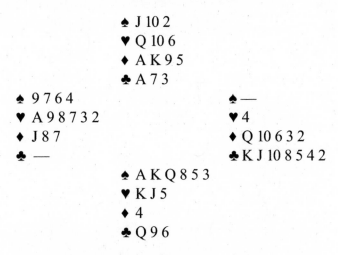

♠ J 10 2
♥ Q 10 6
♦ A K 9 5
♣ A 7 3

♠ 9 7 6 4
♥ A 9 8 7 3 2
♦ J 8 7
♣ —

♠ —
♥ 4
♦ Q 10 6 3 2
♣ K J 10 8 5 4 2

♠ A K Q 8 5 3
♥ K J 5
♦ 4
♣ Q 9 6

"I knew you could do it," my partner says.

The deal provided two lessons for North. First, it's wrong to place your partner with specific cards, no matter how much you want him to have them. There was no reason why I should have held a club singleton (not that slam would have to be a good spot even if I did). If my partner thought slam was possible, he could have consulted me with a 5♣ cue-bid.

Second, to bid close slams at matchpoints is against the odds. If the play requires skill or luck, you'll get a good result for taking 12 tricks whether you're at slam or not. So it proved here. We got a 12, a top, for +1430, but +680 would have been worth 11 1/2. Only a diamond opening lead holds South to 11 tricks.

In a local Swiss Teams, our opponents are strong players. Both sides are vulnerable, and as East I hold

♠ A 8 3
♥ 9 6 4 2
♦ A 5
♣ K Q 10 8

North, the dealer, passes, and I open 1♣. South overcalls 1♦, West responds 1♠ and North passes. I'd rather my spade support were better, but I raise to 2♠. West is likely to have five spades — he didn't respond one heart or 1NT or raise to 2♣ — and I don't like a 1NT rebid with this diamond stopper.

South competes with 3♦, and there are two passes. I can't go any farther with my mediocre spades.

West leads the ♥K, which doesn't look good for us when dummy hits with useful values.

```
              ♠ 10 7 5
              ♥ J 10 7 5
              ♦ 8 6
              ♣ A 6 5 2
                                ♠ A 8 3
                   N            ♥ 9 6 4 2
              W  —+—  E         ♦ A 5
                   S            ♣ K Q 10 8
```

WEST	NORTH	EAST	SOUTH
	Pass	1♣	1♦
1♠	Pass	2♠	3♦
All Pass			

South takes the ♥A and leads the ♦K: four, six .... How can we beat 3♦?

242

I can count one trump, one heart (unless partner took a shot by leading the ♥K from K-x, in which case I see no hope for us) and a spade. If I win and shift to the ♣K, we can set up a club trick or two, or maybe partner has the ♠K or even K-J-x-x.

Before I commit to a line of defense, though, I try to count declarer's shape. Accurate defense without counting is impossible. South surely had at least six diamonds and at least two spades (since West would have competed to 3♠ with a six-card suit). How many hearts? An inference occurs to me: South must have a club loser; if he doesn't, I doubt we have a chance. But if his hearts were A-x, he'd return a heart at the second trick, setting up dummy's J-10 for at least one club pitch. He wouldn't concede a tempo by leading a trump.

So I place South with ♥A83 (or even ♥AQ83), and I see a winning defense. I take the ♦A and return the ♥9 as a suit-preference play. West produces the queen and leads a spade to my ace. He ruffs my heart return with the ♦3, telling me he started with three trumps, and shifts to a club.

South can't avoid losing another trick. He takes dummy's ♣A and throws his last club on the ♥J, but partner still has a trump and ruffs for down one, +100 to us. The full deal:

```
                ♠ 10 7 5
                ♥ J 10 7 5
                ♦ 8 6
                ♣ A 6 5 2
    ♠ J 9 6 4 2                  ♠ A 8 3
    ♥ K Q                        ♥ 9 6 4 2
    ♦ 9 4 3                      ♦ A 5
    ♣ J 7 3                      ♣ K Q 10 8
                ♠ K Q
                ♥ A 8 3
                ♦ K Q J 10 7 2
                ♣ 9 4
```

We gained 5 IMPs. At the other table, East-West took a questionable push to 3♠ over 3♦, and everyone passed. North led the ♦8, and West couldn't quite get home. He lost a diamond, the ♥A, the ♣A and a trump to South's K-Q, and also had to lose a second trump on either an uppercut or a trump promotion. North's ♠10 was a crucial card.

As I See It

Insurance Costs

In a strong IMP game you, North, hold

♠ 10 9 8 3 2
♥ K 8 4
♦ A 8 6 2
♣ K

WEST	NORTH	EAST	SOUTH
		Pass	2♠
Dbl	4♠	5♣	Pass
Pass	?		

Neither side is vulnerable. Do you go to 5♠ or sell out?

My family's insurance costs — especially for health — are high, as I suspect yours may be. We often hear that, in high-level competitive auctions, a player "took out insurance" by bidding one more. The cost of such insurance may not rival that of a major medical plan, but it's hefty enough to demand careful consideration.

When this deal appeared in an expert IMP game, North had to judge.

Dlr: East   ♠ 10 9 8 3 2
Vul: None   ♥ K 8 4
               ♦ A 8 6 2
               ♣ K

♠ Q 7   ♠ —
♥ A Q 7 2   ♥ J 9 6 5 3
♦ Q 10 9   ♦ K 3
♣ A 9 8 3   ♣ Q J 10 7 6 5

               ♠ A K J 6 5 4
               ♥ 10
               ♦ J 7 5 4
               ♣ 4 2

WEST	NORTH	EAST	SOUTH
		Pass	2♠
Dbl	4♠	5♣	Pass
Pass	?		

While North is thinking, let's apply the Law of Total Tricks to this deal. North knows his side has 11 spades. He thinks East-West have at least nine clubs and may have ten. Assuming 21 total trumps, if East-West can make 5♣, North-South will be down only one at 5♠. Perhaps North can beat 5♣ a trick, but then his side will (or so suggests the Law) make 5♠.

All this suggests that North should buy insurance. He has more to gain by bidding than to lose.

But North did no such thing, of course. The Law is no substitute for judgment, and North exercised his. Unless South had one of those magic hands that partners never hold, he wouldn't make 5♠. Against 5♣ North could expect to score the ♦A and the ♥K. He might win a trick with the ♣K, and South might win a spade trick.

Moreover, the cost of insurance was high. If 5♣ made and 5♠ was down one (doubled, presumably), North could gain 7 IMPs by bidding. But if both 5♣ and 5♠ were down one (as was possible if East-West had only a nine-card club fit), North could lose 4 IMPs by bidding.

The odds weren't good enough for North. He passed.

A flaw in the Law is that it assumes perfect play and defense. South led his singleton ♥10, and East grabbed dummy's ace and led the ♠Q. Perhaps this was a "discovery play": East was trying to place the high spades. When North played low, East might indeed have assigned South both the A-K. So I thought East might drop North's ♣K and make 5♣, but he perversely let the ♣Q ride. North produced the king, cashed his ♥K and gave South a heart ruff, and the ♦A had to score for down two.

You can see that 5♠ should also be two down. If West cashes his aces and leads a second heart, South can throw a diamond on the ♥K, draw trumps, strip the clubs and hearts, and lead a diamond to the ace. But if East unblocks his king, avoiding an endplay, South loses two diamonds.

So though there were 21 total trumps, there were, in practice, only 18 tricks. The deal was not a good advertisement for the Law.

Power to the Preempt

1. North-South vulnerable. As West you hold

> ♠ —
> ♥ K 8 5 2
> ♦ J 8 5 2
> ♣ A K 9 8 3

North deals and opens 4♠, and two passes follow. What is your action?

2. Neither side vulnerable. As West you hold

> ♠ Q J 8 7 5 2
> ♥ 6
> ♦ A K 10 9
> ♣ K 6

East deals and opens 1♥, and South overcalls 2♣. You bid 2♠, North jumps to 4♣ (preemptive) and two passes follow. What is your action?

3. Both sides vulnerable. As South you hold

> ♠ A K 10 8 7 3
> ♥ 5
> ♦ A 8 3
> ♣ A 10 3

247

You deal and open 1♠, your partner responds 1NT and East jumps to 4♥. What is your action?

4. North-South vulnerable. As East you hold

♠ 9 6 4
♥ A Q
♦ K Q 10 9 6
♣ Q 10 4

North deals and opens 4♠. You and South pass, and West tries 4NT. North passes. What is your action?

More power to preempts! Here are three deals, all of which appeared the same day in strong internet IMP games.

Dlr: North
Vul: N-S

```
            ♠ A K Q J 8 5 3 2
            ♥ 10 9 7 6
            ♦ —
            ♣ 6
♠ —                         ♠ 9 6 4
♥ K 8 5 2                   ♥ A Q
♦ J 8 5 2                   ♦ K Q 10 9 6
♣ A K 9 8 3                 ♣ Q 10 4
            ♠ 10 7
            ♥ J 4 3
            ♦ A 7 4 3
            ♣ J 7 5 2
```

WEST	NORTH	EAST	SOUTH
	4♠	Pass	Pass
Pass			

East-West could make 6♦, but after North's barrage, most East-Wests never even got into the auction. Neither player had a clear bid. Moreover, East's opening lead against 4♠ was invariably the ♦K, and declarer got rid of his losing club, drew trumps and lost three hearts. (At more than one table, North made an overtrick, presumably after West discarded hearts on the run of the spades.)

At the table I watched, West bravely backed in with a 4NT bid for takeout. I expected East to leap to 6♦ — what his cards were worth

248

— but he settled for 5♦, passed out. He took 12 tricks and might have second-guessed himself for his timid bid, but +420 was better than being -620 against 4♠.

In the next deal, North-South demonstrated that you don't need a hand with eight solid spades to preempt effectively.

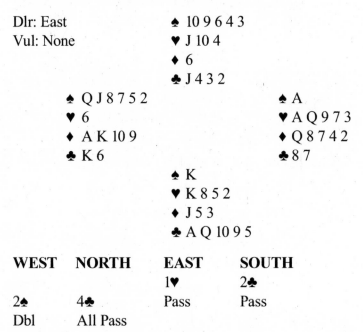

Dlr: East
Vul: None

♠ 10 9 6 4 3
♥ J 10 4
♦ 6
♣ J 4 3 2

♠ Q J 8 7 5 2
♥ 6
♦ A K 10 9
♣ K 6

♠ A
♥ A Q 9 7 3
♦ Q 8 7 4 2
♣ 8 7

♠ K
♥ K 8 5 2
♦ J 5 3
♣ A Q 10 9 5

WEST	NORTH	EAST	SOUTH
		1♥	2♣
2♠	4♣	Pass	Pass
Dbl	All Pass		

Not many North-Souths would have done as well. Not every South would have overcalled 2♣, and not every North would have found the effective preemptive leap to 4♣, as Jimmy Cayne did at the table I watched. East couldn't bid his diamonds freely at the four level, and West, with a singleton heart and a club trick, was willing to take what he could get against 4♣ doubled.

It wasn't much. West led a heart, and East took the ace and erred by cashing the ♠A before returning a heart. West ruffed and next led ... the ♣K. So South lost only one more trick, and East-West were +100, a poor return for their possible slam in diamonds. (As the cards lay, 6♦ was makable with perfect play.)

Preempts work best when they goad an opponent into an unsound action.

```
Dlr: South            ♠ 2
Vul: Both             ♥ 7 4 3
                      ♦ J 10 7 5
                      ♣ K J 8 7 5
      ♠ Q J 5 4                      ♠ 9 6
      ♥ 9 8                          ♥ A K Q J 10 6 2
      ♦ K Q 6 4 2                    ♦ 9
      ♣ 6 4                          ♣ Q 9 2
                      ♠ A K 10 8 7 3
                      ♥ 5
                      ♦ A 8 3
                      ♣ A 10 3
```

At a few tables, the contract was a peaceful partscore in spades or hearts, but at most tables the action was volatile. When North declined to respond to South's 1♠ opening, many Easts reopened with 4♥. They often got doubled and lost 500.

At the table I watched, this was the auction:

WEST	NORTH	EAST	SOUTH
			1♠
Pass	1NT	4♥	4♠
Dbl	All Pass		

If East had passed, South's hand would have been worth 2 5/8 ♠. After the preempt it was worth less — a bad break in spades was likely — and certainly wasn't worth 4♠. Since South had good defensive values, he could expect a plus on defense, and a penalty double of 4♥ would have been wiser. But South let the preempt get his goat, and he conceded 500 instead of collecting that amount.

There is always an aberration to report, and this was the bidding at another table:

WEST	NORTH	EAST	SOUTH
			1♠
Pass	Pass	3♠ (1)	4♠
Dbl	All Pass		

(1) solid suit, asks West to bid 3NT with a spade stopper.

250

Did North-South lose 500 again? Not quite. West, not knowing any better, led a club. South won with the ten and cranked out the ♠AK and a third spade. West won and shifted to a heart, and East won and tried to cash a second heart. (No diamond shift from anybody.) South ruffed, forced out West's last high trump, and later ran the clubs to discard two diamonds for +790.

I Enjoy Being a "Spec"

Log in to OKbridge any evening, and you'll find tables of experts, many with lofty reputations, tuning up their partnerships. Finding such a table is easy. Scroll down the list until you come to one with enough spectators to hold a meeting and elect officers, and you'll find four "names" sitting North, South, East and West.

I'm not sure whether specs watch experts because they take pleasure in good bridge — and hope some of it will rub off — or because they savor bad bridge – and get the warm fuzzies when they see a star player fall on his/her face. I was watching an all-expert IMP game when I and two dozen other specs surveyed this deal:

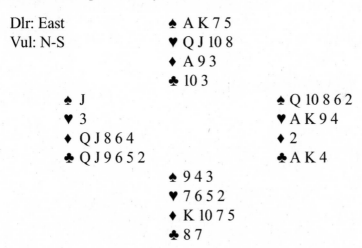

```
Dlr: East        ♠ A K 7 5
Vul: N-S         ♥ Q J 10 8
                 ♦ A 9 3
                 ♣ 10 3
      ♠ J                        ♠ Q 10 8 6 2
      ♥ 3                        ♥ A K 9 4
      ♦ Q J 8 6 4                ♦ 2
      ♣ Q J 9 6 5 2              ♣ A K 4
                 ♠ 9 4 3
                 ♥ 7 6 5 2
                 ♦ K 10 7 5
                 ♣ 8 7
```

A bidding chart would be too cold and impersonal for this one.

Round One: East, 1♠; South, Pass; West, 1NT; North ... Well, it was now or never, and I thought she might double, accepting the risk of a club response. But North produced a disciplined pass.

Round Two: East, 2♥; South, Pass; West ... I know players who would pass for an undoubled penalty at 50 points per undertrick rather than bid again and court utter disaster; but West tried 3♣. And North paused ... and doubled!

This dubious action seemed to confuse the specs. "Is that double for takeout?" one asked.

I could answer that. "No," I typed, "she's going to eat it here." The result was to bear me out.

Round Three: Pass by East, who was no longer concerned with whether to raise the clubs; South, Pass. Add him to the list of confusees.

It looked like +470 to East-West ... but ... West, Huddle. And the longer he thought, the more we knew what was coming. Finally it did. 3♦. Poor West. It did sound as if East had 5-4-3-1 distribution, not 5-4-1-3. North passed.

Round Four: East, 3NT. Hamman's Rule: "If several bids are possible, and 3NT is one of them ..." East could return to 4♣, but it was nobler to go down at game. South, Double. It's not clear what he thought he was going to beat it with, but down one was the likely result.

Unlike the players, the specs were having a fine time, and droll comments abounded.

"Will the real double please stand up?"

"ROFL."

Meanwhile, West with no green suit to bid, passed. North also passed.

Round Five: East, 4♣. Notrump didn't look right anymore. South, Pass; West, Pass; North, Double. South hadn't doubled 4♣, so this double figured to be a small winner or a big loser.

Everyone passed to 4♣ doubled. I expected North to lead a trump, or cash a spade and shift to a trump, but she started with the ♥Q. West took the ♥AK, dispatching his spade loser, and led a diamond. South, hating the whole thing, rose learnedly with the ♦K to shift to a trump.

West proceeded to ruff out North's ♦A, set up the diamonds and draw trumps for 12 tricks, +710.

None of the players made any comment, and I've run out. Let me tell you about the next deal, which was really exciting ...

At My Club

Cy the Cynic, who couldn't find good in a dictionary, views bridge as a microcosm of the trouble the world is in.

"So God created the universe in six days," Cy grunted to me as he slumped over a sandwich in the club lounge one Friday evening. "On the seventh day He must have said, `Okay, Murphy, you take over'."

Cy is a cynic all right – not only absorbed with bitter lessons from his past but preemptively disappointed in his future. I knew he'd been suffering through a run of poor results and was clearly expecting more.

"I can handle a bad board," Cy said sullenly, "but mine aren't merely bad. They're ludicrous."

In his penny Chicago game Cy had cut Millard Pringle, a sweet little man but, unfortunately, not the sharpest tool in the shed.

Dlr: North
Vul: Both

	♠ 8	
	♥ J 4 2	
	♦ A K Q 8 7	
	♣ A K 7 6	
♠ 10 9 7		♠ Q 6 5
♥ —		♥ K Q 10 8 6 3
♦ J 10 9 6 5 4 3 2		♦ —
♣ 9 8		♣ J 10 5 4
	♠ A K J 4 3 2	
	♥ A 9 7 5	
	♦ —	
	♣ Q 3 2	

WEST	NORTH	EAST	SOUTH
	Cy		Millard
	1♦	1♥	1♠
Pass	2♣	Pass	2♥
Pass	3♥	Pass	4♥(!)
Pass	4♠	All Pass	

"What would you bid over 4♥?" Cy asked me.

"3NT," I shrugged, "what I'd have bid over 2♥ if I were playing with Millard for money."

"I panicked," Cy admitted, "but I was sure Millard had long spades and I thought even he might make 4♠."

"What happened?"

"He invented a fun new way to draw trumps. When West led the ♦J, Millard put up the ace and overruffed with his jack when East ruffed. He led a club to dummy and tried the ♦K, and East ruffed again. Millard overruffed, led another club to dummy and returned a third high diamond: ruff, overruff. It then occurred to him to draw trumps by leading one, and West drew them and ran the diamonds. Down five."

"He only dropped eight tricks," I observed. "He's cold for seven, assuming dummy plays low on the opening lead and East forgets to ruff."

"I should have passed 1♠," Cy grumbled. "Then I'd have been minus only 200."

"Actually, your 3♥ was a master call," I said solemnly. "Your mistake was not trusting your partner: you should have let Millard play 4♥. It's unbeatable."

Cy regarded me sourly. "Look, the world is basically fouled up," he said grimly. "There is disorder and disaster all over the place. Tell me how some higher power could have concocted such a mess."

An ancient limerick flitted across my mind:

"God's plan made a hopeful beginning,
But Man spoiled his chances by sinning.
We trust that the story
Will end up in glory,
But at present, the other side's winning.

"And the bridge table," Cy continued resolutely, "is a part of the whole. It's a little sub-plot of imperfection — not to mention boorishness. Now, take Grapefruit: the man is a lock to finish last in the human race."

"You take him," I said. "I don't want him."

"Grapefruit" remains a member of my club only because murder is illegal. He harangues partners incessantly, finding fault as though a reward were offered for it.

"Look at this ridiculousity," Cy said, writing down a deal on his placemat.

```
Dlr: East          ♠ 3
Vul: Both          ♥ A K 9 7 3
                   ♦ K 6
                   ♣ A Q 9 5 4
      ♠ 9 8 6 2              ♠ K 7
      ♥ 10 5 4               ♥ Q J 6 2
      ♦ 7 3                  ♦ A Q 5 2
      ♣ 10 8 6 2             ♣ K J 3
                   ♠ A Q J 10 5 4
                   ♥ 8
                   ♦ J 10 9 8 4
                   ♣ 7
```

WEST	NORTH	EAST	SOUTH
		1NT	2♠
Pass	3♥	Pass	3♠
Pass	4♣	Pass	4♦
Pass	4♠	All Pass	

Cy had watched the deal in a rubber game. Grapefruit was East, and West was a player understandably as nervous as a porcupine in a balloon shop. With no green suit to lead, West tried a diamond. Grapefruit took the queen and ace and led a third diamond, and when South followed, West jerked and ruffed with the ♠2, forgetting that dummy was also out of diamonds. Then three things happened at once: South gleefully overruffed with the three, the phone in the lounge rang and Grapefruit had his say:

"That's your village," he told West, "calling to report their idiot missing."

Unable to finesse in trumps, South continued with the ♣A, club ruff, and A-Q of trumps. Grapefruit won and led a fourth diamond, and West still had a trump and ruffed for the setting trick.

"North pointed out that South would get home if West ruffed high at the third trick," Cy told me, "or if South pitched from dummy instead of overruffing. Grapefruit wasn't impressed: he snarled that West's level of intelligence was proof the gene pool needed some chlorine."

I laughed. "So you've decided this is a hopelessly imperfect game?" I asked Cy.

"I've decided Murphy was an optimist," he growled. He rose and stalked out, leaving his sandwich half-eaten.

****

Saturday found Cy still in a black-ink mood, but he kept a date we had to play in a duplicate. Early on, we met a dentist and a manicurist the club calls "Tooth and Nail" because that's how they argue.

```
Dlr: South        ♠ Q 5
Vul: Both         ♥ 8 6
                  ♦ A 6 4
                  ♣ K Q 10 9 5 2
     ♠ J 8 4 2                    ♠ A K 9 7 6 3
     ♥ J 10 5                     ♥ Q 3
     ♦ K J 9 5                    ♦ 10 7 2
     ♣ 7 3                        ♣ 8 6
                  ♠ 10
                  ♥ A K 9 7 4 2
                  ♦ Q 8 3
                  ♣ A J 4
```

258

WEST	NORTH	EAST	SOUTH
Tooth	me	Nail	Cy
			1♥
Pass	2♣	2♠	3♥
3♠	Pass	Pass	4♣
Pass	4♥	All Pass	

Cy was aghast when he saw dummy — if I'd cue-bid 4♦ instead of showing heart tolerance, we might have reached 6♣ — and he played 4♥ hurriedly. Tooth led the ♠2, and Nail won with the king and shifted to the ♦10. Cy judged correctly to play low from his hand and take dummy's ace. Fearing East might have started with a doubleton diamond, he cashed the top trumps, declining to lead low to his nine, and exited with a trump. Tooth won and led ... another spade, and Cy shrugged and claimed.

The argument broke out immediately.

Nail: "Couldn't you cash your ♦K?"

Tooth: "We'd beat it two if he had another spade."

"Then we'd beat it one anyway, but he couldn't have another spade. With 106,AK9742,Q83,A4 he'd start the clubs after taking the top trumps."

"If you knew the position, discard the ♠A on the third trump to save me from going wrong."

"I found a good shift, and then I have to discard an ace?"

They eventually ran down. Cy sat there all the while, as listless as a condemned man. He threw me a pithy look: everybody and everything was wrong, as usual.

The cards were running East-West, and all day the goddess of chance had her way with the Cynic and me. Finally, on the last round, we reached a pushy notrump game against a competent pair.

```
Dlr: North              ♠ K Q 10 9
Vul: N-S                ♥ K 5
                        ♦ Q J 10 9 7
                        ♣ A 9
        ♠ A 7 6 5                       ♠ J 3
        ♥ Q 9 6 4                       ♥ J 8 7
        ♦ K 5                           ♦ 4 3 2
        ♣ K 7 6                         ♣ Q 10 8 5 3
                        ♠ 8 4 2
                        ♥ A 10 3 2
                        ♦ A 8 6
                        ♣ J 4 2
```

WEST	NORTH	EAST	SOUTH
	me		Cy
	1♦	Pass	1♥
Pass	1♠	Pass	1NT
Pass	2NT	Pass	3NT
All Pass			

West's lead, the ♣6, gave his side a chance. Cy paused for ten seconds and called the nine from dummy.

Give East credit: he found the winning play of the ten – but, alas, not quickly enough to avoid telegraphing his holding. Cy took his jack and led a spade. If the diamonds furnished only four tricks, he needed a spade for the contract. West promptly rose with the ace and led the club king, and when the diamond finesse failed, the result was down one.

"Director!" Cy bellowed when the lie of the cards came to light. Mabel, our club manager, listened to the facts.

"Making five," she ruled. She thought a heart shift was an attractive alternative for West, as did Cy, but East-West snorted their indignation.

I left Cy to cope with an appeal. "It's a litigious world," he said dejectedly as he was led away to face a Committee.

****

The next day was Sunday, and when I got to the club, Cy was there. I thought he looked like Willy Loman at the end of the road.

"Just out of curiosity," I asked, "what'd the Committee do?"

"West told them the winning defense was marked," Cy bit out. "He said that if I'd held Q-J-x in clubs I'd have won the first club with the queen, tempting him to lead the king if he got back in. He also claimed his defense was consistent: he wouldn't have flown with the ♠A unless he planned to lead the ♣K next. The esteemed Committee bought it all and changed the result back to down one. I upchuck."

"Maybe you need a vacation," I said haltingly.

"Don't think I'm not tempted to take a permanent one," the Cynic said in a dull voice. "This place is as ugly as a junkyard."

That afternoon Cy was supposed to partner Ed, a virtuoso player and our club's best, in a ladder match.

"I'm playing with him," Cy had told me earlier, "because I've given up trying to beat him. The man could follow me into a revolving door and come out ahead of me." Nevertheless, Cy sat down with an air of defeat, as if all the rules he'd learned as a child were, one by one, being reversed.

Nothing significant happened for 15 boards. Finesses lost and sometimes won, suits split well and badly, bold vulnerable games made and failed. This was the last board of the half.

```
Dlr: North        ♠ J 9 6 4 2
Vul: N-S          ♥ A 8
                  ♦ A J 10 9
                  ♣ A 4
        ♠ A Q 10               ♠ 8 7 3
        ♥ J 10 9 7 5           ♥ 6 3
        ♦ 8 7 3                ♦ K Q 4 2
        ♣ J 6                  ♣ Q 10 9 8
                  ♠ K 5
                  ♥ K Q 4 2
                  ♦ 6 5
                  ♣ K 7 5 3 2
```

WEST	NORTH	EAST	SOUTH
Ed		Cy	
	1♠	Pass	2♣
Pass	2♦	Pass	2NT
Pass	3NT	All Pass	

I had kibitzed at the other table, where the auction and opening lead — the ♥J — were the same. There, declarer took the ♥A and led a spade: three, king, ace. West shifted to a diamond. Declarer ducked it to the queen, won the heart return and led another spade. West took his queen and led another diamond, and East's king won the defenders' last trick. They were satisfied to hold South to nine tricks; a minor-suit squeeze against East had loomed.

South at Cy's table happened to be my lady Rose. If Grapefruit is our club's ogre, Rose is its angel. Her tact and consideration for partners and opponents alike is admirable. (I think she could tell a man to go to the devil and make him feel proud he was on his way.) Rose's attitude is better than her game, but she strokes a decent dummy. She won the first heart with the ace, huddled and led a spade to her king.

And Ed produced a defense with which I wasn't familiar. He followed in tempo with the queen.

Rose saw no future in the spades, nor was she eager to attack the clubs, where a favorable break seemed unlikely. She tried a diamond to the jack. Cy won and shifted to clubs, knowing Rose had the ♥K as well as the queen since she hadn't let the opening lead ride to her hand. Rose won with the king and took another diamond finesse.

Cy won and forced out the club ace. When Rose cashed dummy's two high diamonds, Ed startled the table by discarding the ♠10. Rose then took the ♥KQ and exited with a club, hoping for an endplay, but East-West had the rest. Down one!

"Did you see that?" Cy said excitedly after everyone realized what had happened.

"Not bad," I mumbled.

"Not bad?" Cy howled, waving his arms. "The play of the decade!"

"That," Rose told Ed graciously, "is the best defensive play I've ever seen."

Cy's team won by 5 IMPs, and afterward, over drinks in the lounge, he was still rhapsodizing about Ed's play.

"Welcome back among the living," I nudged him. He glanced at me, and the gleam in his eyes faded. He lapsed back into brooding mode.

Rose spoke up. She knows the Cynic well, and I'd told her he'd contracted a near-terminal case of disillusionment—not without reason.

"Listen, Cy," Rose said amiably, "I can't explain the chaos in the world any more than I can explain the muddles I make when I'm declarer. The real question is not why evil exists. It's how to account for the presence of so much good. What about the selflessness, the sacrifice, the overcoming adversity? What about all the love?

"You're right," Rose went on, "that bridge is part of a bigger scheme of things. Everything is about falling short. But without the valleys, there would be no mountaintops. There is error and discord and unfairness, but there may be beauty and harmony and grace. What you do is treat the forgettable deals like buzzards and forget 'em – or learn from 'em. But the ones that are unforgettable, you never let go."

Cy's reply was a sigh of resignation. But Monday morning dawned, and that afternoon, sure enough, he was back at the club—still searching for roses among the thorns, still chasing the exhilaration and redemption that one hand can bring.

Valediction

... You have the privilege and pleasure of being part of a community of people with a common interest. Play to win, but never forget that those with whom you contend are not merely "the opponents"; they are friends, or friends yet to be made.

Court them with fellowship and good will and enjoy their company. (They will remember an example of modesty, generosity, conviviality or self-control long after they forget a display of your faultless bidding and play.) In the end, what matters most is not the masterpoints you win and the trophies that rest on your mantle, but how many friendships you make and endeavor to keep ...

– Frank Stewart, responding to the Birmingham Duplicate Bridge Club's gesture of establishing a trophy for a Sectional Swiss Teams in his name.

"If I had to live my life over, I'd live it over a bridge club."
--- Alfred Sheinwold (1912-1997)

About the author

Frank Stewart is one of the world's most prolific bridge journalists. He won many tournament events but discontinued play to devote full time to writing. Stewart served as co-editor of The Bridge BULLETIN 1984-1989 and continues to contribute through the instructional column he began in 1981. He edited the ACBL's World Championship books 1983-1987 and was a principal contributor 1986-1989. He was a principal contributor to the Fifth Edition of "The Official Encyclopedia of Bridge."

In 1986 Stewart began a collaboration with the great Alfred Sheinwold to produce the syndicated newspaper column "Sheinwold on Bridge." After Sheinwold's death in 1997, the column continued under Stewart's byline as "Sheinwold's Bridge" and in 2000 became "Daily Bridge Club." It appears in hundreds of newspapers and on major internet sites.

Stewart has published hundreds of articles in many of the world's leading magazines and on-line publications, including technical pieces, tournament reports, fiction and humor. This is his 20th book. Among the others are "Becoming an Expert," "Frank Stewart's Bridge Club," and "My Bridge and Yours." He is a frequent analyst for ACBL-wide charity events.

Stewart is a graduate of the University of Alabama where he studied voice and musicology. He is a low-handicap golfer and a past chairman of the Fayette AL Christian Center of Concern, a food bank. He and his wife Charlotte, a pediatric speech-language pathologist, live in Fayette AL. They have a seven year old daughter.